My Words

My Words

Alan Litherland

'Heaven and Earth will pass away; my words will never pass away.'

Mark 13: 31

EPWORTH PRESS

FIRST PUBLISHED IN 1968 BY
EPWORTH PRESS
Book Steward: Frank H. Cumbers
PRINTED IN GREAT BRITAIN BY
PAGE & THOMAS
THE CHESHAM PRESS LIMITED
CHESHAM, BUCKINGHAMSHIRE
SBN 7162 0060 0

Contents

Preface

THIS book is not the work of a theologian or a Biblical scholar, but of a layman with a scientific background, studying the Bible as honestly as possible and expressing a layman's point of view.

It began some years ago when I decided to read the Gospels through again in a modern language version. As one who had been a lay preacher in the Methodist Church for many years, the thought which was increasingly thrust upon me by this exercise was: 'This is not Methodism!' Nor, for that matter, is it Anglicanism or Roman Catholicism. In other words—as many others must have observed before—the content of Christ's teaching, especially as it is recorded in the synoptic Gospels, is in some respects remarkably at variance with the 'Christianity' of the traditional churches.

On further study the original thought grew into a theme of which the focal point was the simple proposition that the primary authority for the Christian faith is Christ. The churches have added much to his teaching which, whatever its value may have been in the past, is not necessarily relevant today. My plea is that, at this time of ferment in Christian thinking, when we are seeking to apprehend and present the truth of Christ in a way which meets the need of our present age, we should put the teaching of Christ himself in the centre.

I am not at present concerned with the application of his teaching to the ethics of everyday life or social problems, important though that is, but chiefly with the theological side—the Christian faith rather than the Christian way of life. Much of what I have to say will be familiar ground to the expert. It needs to be said however, because it is an essential part of the argument, and in any case is certainly not familiar ground to many Christians.

Because I know no Hebrew or Greek and only a smattering of Church history, I may have drawn conclusions which those with wider knowledge would consider unjustified. But I am convinced that the main points are straightforward enough not to depend on extensive background knowledge or subtlety of interpretation. All New Testament quotations in the book are in the words of the New English Bible, to which I owe a debt of gratitude. Those from the Old Testament are in the words of the American Revised Standard Version.

My thanks are due to many friends better qualified than myself, whose kindly criticisms have helped me to avoid obvious mis-statements and, I trust, to express the theme more effectively.

1 The Authority of Christ

'What then of the man who hears these words of mine and acts upon them? He is like a man who had the sense to build his house on rock.' Matthew 7: 24

ONE way of silencing a troublesome worker is to promote him. One way of rendering an outspoken politician harmless is to elevate him to the House of Lords, where wise people can say wise things without the need to take too much notice of what they say.

It is something like this that the Church has done to Jesus. In His lifetime He was an outspoken revolutionary who was so troublesome that the authorities conspired to get rid of Him. To His contemporaries He was either a teacher and healer, or a dangerous firebrand, according to their point of view; but to the Church, believing in Him as the risen Christ, He became Lord and God. To His contemporaries the things He said were sometimes subversive and often devastating; to us they have become respectable and almost innocuous, partly because they are so familiar, but partly because His elevation from teacher to Lord has reduced the impact of His words.

Logically, to emphasize the divinity of Christ should make His teaching seem all the more authoritative and important, but human nature is not made that way. It is possible to put a man on such a high pedestal that you miss what he is saying. To those around Him, one of the most remarkable things about Jesus was that He taught as one having authority; but the Church, by making faith in Christ as Lord the central point of its doctrine, has unavoidably pushed the authority of His words out of the centre and made them relatively less important. To worship

Christ as Lord can be a means of escape from the unwelcome or unpleasant things He said. No doubt many Christian leaders have been conscious of this danger, but it is still with us, as it was when Jesus Himself said, according to Luke, 'Why do you keep calling me "Lord, Lord" and never do what I tell you?'

In every sphere of life we need authorities. No one can discover everything for himself and most of us rely, even in our own specialist field, on the wisdom, experience and insight of others, especially those who have become recognized as authorities. This applies to religion as much as to other subjects, and my first proposition is that for the Christian faith the primary authority should be Christ himself. Let us consider that authority in two aspects.

Jesus spoke with authority about human conduct, morals and relationships, and what He said was both revolutionary and difficult to accept. In our respectable twentieth-century Christianity, we have contrived to ignore or drastically modify some of this teaching, but I do not propose to enter into that here.

Jesus was also an authoritative theologian. He spoke with authority about God, man, sin and eternal life, as well as about some of the implications of those truths in matters of worship and ritual observance. It is with this aspect of His authority that the present book is concerned.

Whatever one may think about the divisions and dogmas of Christendom, one of the greatest things the churches have done down the ages is to collect, preserve and pass on with quite extraordinary faithfulness the best available records of what He said and did. If we are Christians, then the centre of our faith and life should be to 'hear these words of mine and act upon them'—as far as we know them from the records. It should be noted, by the way, that the 'rock' referred to in the quotation at the head of this chapter signifies not Christ himself, but His words.

Having said this,we must hasten to add two qualifications.

In the first place, our record of the teaching of Jesus is

incomplete, in the sense that He must have said a great deal which is not included in our Bible. Indeed, it may well be that the apostles remembered and took account of many sayings of Jesus which did not become part of the 'standard' oral traditions, later to be written down in our Gospels. But, more important than this, the significance of His death and resurrection, which the apostles put in the centre of their preaching, could—by its very nature—only be touched upon in the record of His own words. Inevitably, therefore, the apostles had something fundamental and important to add to the original teaching of the Master; and later Christians, in response to new situations and new experience, would also be able to add new facets to a faith which—though grounded in an historical person—need not be fixed or static. Nevertheless, if our faith is still to be called by the name of Christ, then everything added at any stage must always be in line with and in keeping with His own words. These remain our primary authority, though not our only one.

In the second place, the words of Jesus were couched in the idiom of His time, expressed in images which would be meaningful to the people of His time, and had their significance against the background of life in the Middle East 1900 years ago. We may therefore need to re-interpret or perhaps modify the original teaching to make it significant and truthful for our own time. But if our re-interpretation leads to ideas which are basically different from that original teaching, then it is scarcely honest to call those ideas 'Christian'.

It may seem unnecessary thus to emphasize the primary authority of Christ and His teaching, and the immediate reaction of some may be: 'But of course! Whoever suggested anything else?' Unfortunately Christian leaders have sometimes stated and often implied a quite different principle. We will begin with a brief reference to three publications which express official doctrines of the churches and are intended for reading by lay people.

First, the Roman Catholic Church: the Catholic Enquiry

Centre in London publishes a course of 21 leaflets explaining the Catholic faith and summarizing the grounds for Catholic beliefs and doctrines. Throughout these documents the authority of Christ is acknowledged as paramount. One has the impression that His teaching forms the framework around which the whole complex structure of doctrine is built, and as each doctrine is explained the reasoning begins, in almost every case, with some consideration of the words of Jesus as recorded in the Gospels. Nevertheless the development of many of the doctrines travels such a long way from that starting point that it needs a great effort of imagination to believe that the final conclusion is 'in line with and in keeping with' the words of Jesus. But we shall return to that later.

A corresponding series of leaflets is issued on behalf of the Free Churches by the Christian Enquiry Bureau. Here the primary authority of Christ for Christian thinking is also specifically stated and emphasized, though in their consideration of the content and implications of the Christian faith they do not give the same impression of constantly referring to Jesus as standard. For the most part the connexion with His teaching is less explicitly stated than in the Catholic publication, and yet the net result seems more closely related to it—but perhaps that is just a non-Catholic's point of view.

A very different picture is presented by the Report of the Conversations between the Church of England and the Methodist Church, published in 1963. This was written with particular reference to the proposals for union of the two churches, and was not intended as a summary of Christian doctrine. One of its purposes, however, was to show how the two churches were already very close in their fundamental beliefs, and for this reason the report deals with questions of authority and doctrine at some length. Yet the teaching of Jesus is scarcely referred to at all and is nowhere acknowledged as having any sort of overriding authority for the Christian or the Church.

The chapter on 'Scripture and Tradition' deals with the sources of authority for Christian beliefs and practice, and lists three such authorities in order of importance: the Holy Scriptures; the faith and practice of the very early Church; and the developing tradition of the churches in later years. The teaching of Jesus is neither quoted nor referred to. In the two subsequent chapters, on 'Gospel, Church Order and Ministry' and 'The Sacraments', there are summarized many doctrines, practices and duties worked out by people other than Jesus, and expressed in terms originating from people other than Jesus; but there is again no reference to the words of Jesus Himself, save by implication in the statement that 'The sacraments of Baptism and Holy Communion are sacraments of the Gospel and derive their authority from Christ Himself'.

This remarkable omission of any direct reference to the authoritativeness of the teaching of Christ may be quite unintentional and partly due to the difficulties of expressing things briefly. Yet the general tenor of these brief statements of doctrine implies that the Christian faith is mainly concerned with what St. Paul and other New Testament writers have taught *about* Christ, rather than with what Christ taught Himself. This emphasis seems to be characteristic of 'evangelical' Christianity and it illustrates one of the main divergences from Christ's teaching which can be traced right back to the early days of the Church. Though the other two publications referred to do acknowledge the primary authority of Christ, yet they include ideas and doctrines which also diverge considerably from His teaching. In the next chapter we shall begin to enquire how some of the divergences arose.

2 The Development of Divergences

AROUND the original teaching of Jesus a complex structure of doctrine, tradition and practice has been built. It is not possible for a layman to trace in detail the developing thought of the central tradition, or the various divisions and divergences from that tradition which have inevitably occurred down the ages. Perhaps, however, the very complexity of the developments makes it all the more necessary to pick out a few well-known salient features which show the greatest differences and to ask why these differences occurred.

According to the synoptic Gospels, Jesus, the son of a carpenter, went about Palestine healing the sick, casting out demons and preaching the good news of the kingdom of God. He offered forgiveness to repentant sinners and taught a new way of life of which the keynote was carefree trust in God and love of one's neighbour. He set a very high standard of personal morality and warned that His followers would suffer persecution. He let it be known to those who could understand that He was the promised Messiah and that He would be done to death by the authorities, but that after catastrophic wars and sufferings He, the Son of Man, would come again soon to establish God's everlasting kingdom.

According to the Bible records, after the death and resurrection of Jesus, the apostles took up the work where He had left off, but from the beginning of their preaching there was an immediate and startling change of emphasis. As the Acts of the Apostles was written by Luke as a continuation of his record of the life and teaching of Jesus, it is legitimate to compare the content of the preaching in Acts with the preaching of Jesus as recorded in Luke's

Gospel, thus avoiding any differences which might be due to the point of view of the author. Briefly, instead of continuing to teach what He taught—as one would normally expect the disciples of a great teacher to do—they seemed to confine themselves almost exclusively to preaching *about* Him.

Luke's record of Jesus' brief ministry includes teaching on a very wide variety of subjects—theological, ethical and pragmatic: God's loving care for individuals, His free forgiveness for repentant sinners, the transforming and healing power of the 'kingdom of God', the various parables of the kingdom, the upside-down values of the kingdom, the supreme worthwhileness of entering into the new life of the kingdom, the 'impossibly' high standards of honesty, purity, humility, helpfulness, forgiveness which the life of the kingdom demands, the danger of riches, the efficacy of faith, the error of outward observances and traditional restrictionisms, the great commandments of love to God and one's neighbour, the sacredness of marriage, the need for persistent prayer and seeking after goodness, the warnings of persecution and catastrophe . . . and many others.

Hardly any of this finds mention in the early teaching of the apostles as it is summarized in Acts. There is scarcely any reference to the words of Jesus and the preaching is focused on one simple message which, in the form intended for Jewish hearers, may be summarized in Peter's words:

'Let all Israel then accept as certain that God has made this Jesus, whom you crucified, both Lord and Messiah . . . Repent and be baptized, every one of you, in the name of Jesus the Messiah for the forgiveness of your sins; and you will receive the gift of the Holy Spirit.'

In preaching to Gentiles, of course, the message had to be modified, but the general theme seems to have been the same; thus Paul at Athens:

'Now he commands mankind, all men everywhere, to repent, because he has fixed the day on which he will have the world judged, and justly judged, by a man of his choosing; of this he has given assurance to all by raising him from the dead.'

One reason for the change of emphasis is clear enough. The apostles were speaking to people who did not yet accept the authority of Christ, and necessarily the first objective of their public preaching was to proclaim and establish that authority. As the early Church expanded and became a force to be reckoned with, the issue for the Jews was a simple one: to accept or reject the claim that Jesus was Lord and Messiah. Therefore, inevitably, the apostles' testimony centred upon that claim.

Most great teachers, such as Plato or Aristotle, have established their authority mainly by the content of their teaching, and their followers succeeding them have passed on the teaching, often with persistent literalness, on the basis of that authority. But the apostles, in seeking to establish the authority of Jesus, did not even mention His teaching as part of the evidence, and based their case on three quite different arguments:

1. The prophecies of Old Testament scripture fulfilled in Jesus;
2. The miracles of Jesus: 'A man singled out by God and made known to you through miracles, portents and signs, which God worked among you through him, as you well know'; and
3. The resurrection of Jesus, setting the seal of divine authority.

The reason for this is fairly plain: they were not advertising Jesus as a teacher, but as a saviour, and as the only saviour: 'There is no salvation in anyone else at all, for there is no other name under heaven granted to men, by which we may receive salvation'—a claim, by the way, which the Jesus of the synoptic Gospels does not seem to have made for Himself.

This is not to imply that the apostles ignored the teaching

of Jesus. Indeed, in their life, fellowship, dedication, prayer and healing ministry they lived it out—as nearly as anyone has ever done—to the letter; and one may presume that His words and deeds, His parables and sermons, formed a large part of their devotions together and the teaching they gave to new converts entering the Church. Why, then, was it apparently omitted so pointedly from their public preaching?

This is a question to which we can only guess the answer, but the omission becomes less surprising when one remembers what it was which so completely revolutionized their lives. For two or three years they had followed Him, loved Him and looked to Him for leadership. They had seen His power, heard His parables, tried to understand His teaching and tried to live with His goodness—but all this had not transformed their lives, nor made them fit to carry on His work. Only after His resurrection did the whole thing fall into place. The divine vindication of His authority which the resurrection meant to them, and the experience of His risen presence with them, changed them from inadequate and sometimes perplexed followers to triumphantly courageous witnesses. His teaching had trained them in a new kind of faith in God and a new way of life; His resurrection commissioned them to go out and preach. Small wonder that the fact of His resurrection was central in their preaching; and that they practised His teaching while they preached His saving power. This was the basis of the spread of Christian faith from then on, and became, with various modifications, the theme of the central tradition of the Christian churches. Indeed, the faith of the churches is often proudly called the 'apostolic faith', a reminder that it is not, in fact, the faith preached by Jesus, but the faith preached by the apostles about Jesus.

This new emphasis apparent in the apostolic preaching is also central in the writings of Paul, the earliest writings of the New Testament as we have it today, and in some ways the theology of Paul re-emphasized the divergence between the 'apostolic faith' and what we know of the original teaching of Jesus. Again, it is not difficult to see reasons for this. Jesus condemned outward observances and the Pharisees who set so much store by them. Paul had been brought up as one of those Pharisees and we may guess that his zeal for every detail of the law had been the equal of any. Yet all that zeal for the law had not brought him fulfilment, and it was the vivid experience of Christ at his conversion which transformed his whole life—a far more sudden and radical change than that experienced by the other apostles, who had been 'on the side of' Jesus from the beginning of His ministry.

Inevitably, Paul must have felt that the whole of his former life was under condemnation, in spite of all the good intentions and obedience to the law which he may have achieved; and that the blinding experience which brought him faith in Christ was the one thing which stood between himself and the condemnation of God. In contrast to Paul's conviction and experience, there were Jewish Christians who wanted to preserve the Pharisaic approach and to tie the new faith to the old observances of the law. To do this would surely have split the Church and perhaps done irreparable harm to the cause.

So the first seven chapters of Paul's letter to the Romans are concerned with the question of justification—avoiding the just condemnation of God—and he brings to bear all the authority he can muster in support of his thesis that faith in Christ is the one thing that matters. In developing this theme he gives a wealth of quotation from scripture—yet never a single one from the words of Christ himself.

Again, I am not suggesting for one moment that St. Paul ignored the teaching of Jesus in general. Some of the best-known passages in his letters, such as Romans 12 and I Corinthians 13, are saturated with the spirit of that teaching, but these are concerned with ethics rather than theology. In developing his characteristic theological doctrines, which have exercised such a profound influence on Christian thinking ever since, he does not seem to have gone to the words of Christ for guidance; rather he was concerned to fit the supreme fact of Christ, as revealed in his own and the other apostles' personal experience, into the pattern of Old Testament thought. Even allowing for the fact that he was a Jew writing to Jews and appealing to the authority of Old Testament teachings in the customary way, it is remarkable that for him the teaching of Jesus had not yet assumed the same authoritative importance as 'scripture'. Again and again he quotes scripture as authoritative, but never once does he suggest that Jesus may have had something useful to say on matters of theology. The omission may be partly explained in terms of the circumstances of the letters and the people to whom they were written, but these circumstances do not seem to have been taken into account when his theological arguments were converted into formal doctrines of the churches.

The same reluctance to appeal to the authority of Jesus is even more apparent in the letter to the Hebrews, which is thought to have been written about the same time as Mark's Gospel. While in the well-known twelfth chapter the writer bids us keep 'our eyes fixed on Jesus, on whom faith depends from start to finish', he does not himself consult the teaching of Jesus for guidance on the subject-matter of his letter. Though he adduces something like 35 quotations from Old Testament scripture in support of his reasoning, and illustrates it with many incidents from the lives of the fathers of Israel, there is not a single word from the teaching of Jesus. One could read the whole thirteen chapters of this epistle without gaining an inkling that the Christ who is the centre of its theme ever actually taught anything at all.

As with Paul's writings and the early preaching of the apostles, there were no doubt good reasons for this particular emphasis, but all these things contribute to a remarkable dichotomy in New Testament thinking. In matters of Christian behaviour and morals the New

Testament writers faithfully followed the example and teaching of Jesus. But in matters of theology—apart from the four Gospels—they almost entirely passed by His words as if on this subject He had nothing important to say. Instead of seeking guidance from Him they based their conclusions on Old Testament patterns and wove them round Jesus as a sort of figurehead. The result is that an important part of the doctrinal preaching of the churches, based as it is on the 'apostolic faith', diverges considerably from the teaching of Jesus as we know it.

Soon after the death of St. Paul the earliest of the four Gospels was written—that of Mark, in about A.D. 65. Then, a few years later, came Luke's Gospel and the Acts of the Apostles and, later still, Matthew's Gospel. During the early spread of Christianity there had been a sense of urgency and immediate crisis—an expectation of the 'end of the age' and the second coming of Christ—which must have made the writing of records seem rather unnecessary. But by the time of Paul's death, more than thirty years after the death of Jesus, it was becoming apparent that a more long-term view was necessary, and there was a need to put on record the facts about Jesus, what He did and said, while there were still eye-witnesses living to tell the tale.

In a sense these three Gospels form a counterweight to the writings of Paul in our New Testament. The fourth Gospel, on the other hand—probably written 60 to 80 years after the death of Jesus, represents a move back towards the 'apostolic' emphasis. There are so many sharp differences between the account of Jesus' teaching here and that found in the synoptic Gospels that it is not possible to accept both as literal records of the actual words of the Master. It is generally accepted that the author, a deep thinker and theologian who had meditated upon his faith for many years, allowed his own convictions to enter into the record. The Gospel thus became not only a new account of the ministry, death and resurrection of Jesus, but also a theological treatise on the significance of it all. The author therefore, with his own characteristic slant, achieved a kind of synthesis between the apostolic faith about Jesus and the teaching of Jesus Himself.

We have considered something of the different emphases characterizing those New Testament books which have contributed most to the development of faith and doctrine in the Christian churches down the ages: at the one extreme the 'primitive' teaching of the Jesus of the synoptic Gospels and at the other the developed theology of St. Paul and the writer to the Hebrews, with the synthesis of the fourth Gospel as a connecting link between the two. When, sometime before A.D. 367, the selection of books in the New Testament as we have it today was finally decided upon, a balance was achieved—whether by conscious design or not—between those different emphases. To this extent the New Testament presents a coherence of thought in spite of its divergences. The divergences did, however, create difficulties which have often been glossed over—but we shall see more of that later.

Divergences of other kinds began to develop when the Christian Church survived persecution and minority status and became an established and powerful institution.

One of the most difficult tasks of Christian leaders down the ages must have been to maintain the continuity of the faith and prevent the rise of all sorts of false or independent teachings which would not only lead sincere people astray but also cause conflict and division within the 'body of Christ'. It was therefore evidently necessary to define the nature of the faith in a fairly precise way in accordance with the early teaching of the apostles, and to endeavour to hold all believers to this established definition. From time to time some new idea would arise which was deemed by the main body of Christian thought to be heretical, so that a new definition or clarification of the true faith became necessary. Thus developed a complex system of defined dogma—re-defined or added to from time to time—of the kind which is characteristic of the Roman Catholic Church today.

The teaching of Jesus in the synoptic Gospels was to a large extent 'free', being expressed mainly in illustrative or pictorial ways, but with some basic truths bluntly stated from time to time. There were few tidy definitions or theological dogmas. The later development of detailed, systematic doctrines, therefore, however good the intentions behind them, represented a progressive movement away from the original 'informality' of Jesus.

Another aspect of this formalism, on the more popular level, was the occurrence of what one might call 'ticket to heaven' religion—the idea that spiritual benefits could be purchased by fulfilling ritual observances or even paying monies to a priest. We shall return to this later.

What we know as the Reformation represented in one sense a swing of the pendulum away from excessive emphasis on outward form and back to the apostolic faith. Against the authority of a wealthy, powerful and sometimes ruthless Church the reformers wielded the authority of the Bible. Against the pre-occupation with outward form and ticket-to-heaven religion, such as paying money for indulgences, they brought to bear the authority of Paul and his doctrine of salvation through faith. It is interesting to note here that in the relevant teaching of Jesus the antithesis was between outward form and inward spirit, while in the Pauline and evangelical doctrine it was between 'works' and faith—which is not quite the same thing. Be that as it may, the result was that the reforms became centred on the authority of scripture and the characteristic doctrines of Paul as outlined in his letter to the Romans.

As a result of these and many other developments in the long and chequered history of the Christian faith, there seem to be in Christendom today two main kinds of theological divergence from the original teaching of Jesus. One might call them the formalistic divergence, with its elaboration of dogma, rule and ritual observance, and the evangelical divergence with its undue emphasis on some of Paul's theology. These divergences appear in many different forms and add up to a serious movement away from Christ. It might therefore be a good thing if we could start at the beginning again, acknowledging the primary authority of Christ and applying and interpreting His teaching to our generation, as the early apostles applied it and interpreted Him to theirs.

3 The Presumption of Biblical Unity

EVERY religion depends to a greater or lesser extent upon its records, and Christianity is to a very large extent a religion of the Bible. The Christian churches believe that the nature and will of God was revealed uniquely in Christ; the record of the life, teaching, death and resurrection of Jesus is therefore of supreme importance to the faith, if not indispensable. But the Bible contains much more than this, and it is the Bible as a whole, rather than the mere record of Jesus, which has been given supreme authority as a library of sacred truth. To quote the Anglican-Methodist Report of 1963: 'The Holy Scriptures are the inspired witness to the revelation of God, and constitute the supreme rule of faith'. It seems to me that this habit of thinking of the Bible as a unitary whole, and the tacit presumption that it speaks infallibly and with one voice ('the word of God'), has been and still is one of the most serious errors of the Christian churches.

This is so important that it is necessary to dwell at some length upon the divergent voices of the Bible, even at the risk of boring those who are perfectly aware of them already.

We are all familiar with the fact that the Bible records a progressive development of religious faith and thought. In particular, it records quite revolutionary changes in man's thinking about the nature and character of God, from the glorified human being 'walking in the garden in the cool of the day' to the unimaginable creator of all things who 'sits upon the circle of the earth, and its inhabitants are like grasshoppers'; from the God of battles who ordered His people invading Palestine to kill women and children mercilessly and to the bitter end to the loving heavenly

Father who cares for two sparrows falling to the ground and bids us love our enemies. Indeed, Jesus himself emphasized this progression of thought when he boldly stated new principles which went far beyond, or even contradicted, the commonly accepted thinking of the Old Testament: 'You have learned that they were told "An eye for an eye and a tooth for a tooth." But what I tell you is this. . .'

Apart from this progressive development of ideas in the course of time, there are in the Old Testament two main conflicting streams of religious thought which run side by side—the prophetic or radical approach and the priestly or conservative approach. Both streams showed progressive development, and the prophetic to quite a large extent influenced the priestly, but fundamentally they were always in conflict with one another and often the conflict became vigorous and open. Yet both are set forth side by side in the Old Testament.

Probably the biggest source of conflict was the question of ritual and sacrifices. The first seven chapters of Leviticus are devoted almost exclusively to describing what kind of sacrifices ought to be made, through the mediation of the priests, in all sorts of circumstances. These laws were said to have been given by God to Moses and formed the basis of the sacrificial ritual which was still in operation at the time of Christ.

Leviticus is part of 'The Law', the first five books of our Bible, which right up to the time of Christ were regarded as having greater authority than any other writings of the Hebrew scriptures. Yet most of the great prophets condemned sacrificial ritual and said that God did not want it:

Amos 5: 21.

'I hate, I despise your feasts,
and I take no delight in your solemn assemblies.
Even though you offer me your burnt offerings and cereal offerings,
I will not accept them,

and the peace offerings of your fatted beasts
I will not look upon . . .'
'Did you bring me sacrifices and offerings the forty years in the wilderness, O house of Israel?'

Hosea 6: 6.
'For I desire steadfast love and not sacrifice,
the knowledge of God rather than burnt offerings.'

Isaiah 1: 11.
'What to me is the multitude of your sacrifices?'
says the Lord;
'I have had enough of burnt offerings or rams
and the fat of fed beasts;
I do not delight in the blood of bulls,
or of lambs, or of he-goats.'

Micah 6: 6.
'Shall I come before him with burnt offerings
with calves of a year old?
Will the Lord be pleased with thousands of rams,
with ten thousand rivers of oil?'
'He has showed you, O man, what is good;
and what does the Lord require of you
but to do justice and to love kindness,
and to walk humbly with your God.'

Jeremiah 7: 22.
'For in the day that I brought them out of the land of Egypt, I did not speak to your fathers or command them concerning burnt offerings and sacrifices. But this command I gave them, 'Obey my voice, and I will be your God, and you shall be my people . . .'

There could scarcely be a more emphatic confrontation of opposite points of view, each claiming to come direct from God, on a subject which was central to the religious life of the Hebrews.

Jesus, in much of his teaching, was in direct line with the prophets rather than the priests, but He does not seem to have condemned sacrifices as such. When He quoted Hosea's 'I desire mercy, and not sacrifice', He was referring to ritual observance of the Sabbath rather than to burnt offering.

A third kind of disagreement in the Bible is shown in discrepancies between different records of the same events —discrepancies which are natural and reasonable when one recognizes that different authors and different sources of information are involved.

For example, there are two irreconcilable accounts of creation in Genesis, and there is surely nothing unreasonable about this. It seems natural and sensible for the editors of the book, having two differing records at their disposal and not knowing which to choose, to put them both in side by side.

Similar discrepancies due to two or more different sources keep appearing in later parts of the Old Testament. In one account of the flood the animals are taken into the Ark in pairs; in the other Noah chooses the clean beasts and birds by sevens and the other animals by pairs. In one story of Joseph's expulsion his brothers sold him to a party of Ishmaelites; in the other he was kidnapped by Midianites. In one account of the sacred tent carried by the children of Israel in the wilderness it was an elaborate construction served by more than 8000 Levites; in another it was a simple affair looked after by a single Ephraimite. In one account of the anointing of Saul, Samuel is a local prophet who, guided by God, anoints Saul in private, the tribes later proclaiming him king after his success in battle; in another, Samuel is a national figure who, under pressure from the people and against God's 'better judgement', arranges for the king to be chosen by lot.

Often the discrepancies are traceable to the differing opinions of the authors or editors, especially in the two accounts of the same periods of history, written with very different bias, in Chronicles and in Samuel-Kings. For example, there are two accounts of David's census, almost word for word the same except that one (2 Samuel 24: 1) states that the Lord incited David to do it, whereas the other (1 Chronicles 21: 1) states that Satan incited him!

In the New Testament the same kind of differing narratives may be found: discrepancies which may be attributed to errors in memory or recording, and differing versions which express the differing convictions of the authors.

In the four accounts of the resurrection of Jesus there are a number of irreconcilable differences of detail which—to anyone but a literal fundamentalist—strengthen rather than weaken the reliability of the record, because they show that we have honest accounts obtained from different sources rather than versions which have been copied or made to fit in with one another. One detail in which all four versions differ is the description of the visit of the women to the tomb—which of the women went and what they found when they got there; Matthew, always the romantic one, is the only one of the four who mentions guards, an earthquake or an angel rolling away the stone and sitting upon it.

Minor discrepancies of this kind, though they make nonsense of any idea of literal divine inspiration imparting word-for-word infallibility to statements in scripture, do not invalidate the reliability of the record from any reasonable point of view. There are, however, much more fundamental differences in the Gospels which present a serious difficulty. The behaviour, manner and teaching of the Jesus of the fourth Gospel is quite different from that of the records in Matthew, Mark and Luke, though there are one or two brief 'Johanine' passages embedded in the synoptic Gospels, such as Luke 10: 22. The teaching of the Jesus of the fourth Gospel is, in comparison with the other three, consistently and coherently biased in favour of the author's aim, as stated in John 20: 31: 'That you may hold the faith that Jesus is the Christ, the Son of God, and that through this faith you may possess eternal life by his name.'

Consistent with the first part of this aim, the Jesus of the fourth Gospel publicly claims to be the Messiah, the Son of God, and dwells on the significance of this relationship on many occasions, especially in a series of arguments with 'the Jews', both in Galilee and in Jerusalem. In the synoptic Gospels, on the other hand, Jesus refers to Himself enigmatically as 'Son of Man' rather than 'Son of God'. He is at pains to let people draw their own conclusions about His Messiahship, and to tell them to keep it dark when they have made the discovery. Even in the last days, in the triumphal entry He acts rather than announces His Messiahship, and at the enquiry by the Sanhedrin carefully leaves the phrase 'Son of God' open to doubt.

Turning to the second part of John's declared aim: 'That through this faith you may possess eternal life by his name', we find that this theme, too, has been put into the mouth of Jesus in a way which is completely absent from the teaching of the Jesus of the synoptic Gospels. The theme of eternal life is frequently mentioned in the synoptics, and on two occasions Jesus is asked the straight question, 'What must I do to inherit eternal life?' His answer is broadly the same in both cases: keep the commandments and be good to those in need. In the parable of the sheep and the goats eternal life is, again, the reward for helpfulness. Nowhere does Jesus say that eternal life is attained through faith—either in Himself or in God.

Consistent with this emphasis on Christ's Sonship and the central importance of faith in Him, the Jesus of the fourth Gospel develops the same theme in the great 'I ams'—the vivid, metaphorical claims with which He describes His own rôle in the new life which is offered to those who put their faith in Him:

6: 35. 'I am the bread of life. Whoever comes to me shall never be hungry, and whoever believes in me shall never be thirsty.'

8: 12. 'I am the light of the world. No follower of mine shall wander in the dark; he shall have the light of life.'

10: 7-9. 'I am the door of the sheepfold. . . . anyone who comes into the fold through me shall be safe. He shall go in and out and shall find pasturage.'

10: 11. 'I am the good shepherd; the good shepherd lays down his life for the sheep.'

11: 25. 'I am the resurrection and I am life. If a man has faith in me, even though he die, he shall come to life.'

14: 6. 'I am the way; I am the truth and I am life; no one comes to the Father except by me.'

15: 1. 'I am the real vine, and my Father is the gardener. Every barren branch of mine he cuts away; and every fruiting branch he cleans, to make it more fruitful still.'

Not one of these sayings, nor anything resembling them, appears in any of the synoptic Gospels. It is generally accepted that these Gospels were written much earlier than the fourth, and that the compilers made use of oral or written material handed down from the apostles, now thought to have been in the form of separate, self-contained 'units' used for teaching and preaching in the Church. If Jesus really did make these magnificent and unforgettable utterances about Himself, which could not possibly be regarded as unimportant, it is inconceivable that the three Gospel writers should forget them, or be unaware of them, or consider them so unimportant as to omit all reference to them. We are left, therefore, with a wide and fundamental contradiction between the synoptic and the Johanine accounts of how Jesus behaved and what He said.

To sum up, the Bible is not to be thought of as a unit, but as a whole library of religious writings covering many hundreds of years. It embodies quite revolutionary changes in men's ideas on the nature of God and what He requires of us; it contains in many places differing and irreconcilable records of the same events; it includes in the Old Testament two conflicting and irreconcilable views on the central question of service to God, both proclaimed as having God's authority; it offers in the New Testament two differing and irreconcilable versions of the teaching of Jesus; and there are also many discrepancies in detail which are usually unimportant and sometimes strengthen rather than weaken the reliability of the record.

In most religions there is a tendency for ideas which were originally fluid to become crystallized and fixed—sometimes to the detriment of the original truths—and in Christianity this crystallization overtook the Bible, until a particular collection of books covering a wide divergence of viewpoint became known as 'The Word of God'. Even some of the books of our Old Testament were not recognized as having the authority of scripture until well after the time of Christ; while for something like two centuries there was considerable doubt as to which New Testament books should be regarded as canonical, and it was only in the fourth century that the content of the New Testament as we have it today was finally accepted.

In spite of this prolonged uncertainty about which books should be included, the authoritativeness of the whole Bible became established in due course as a matter of dogma, and apparently for many centuries Christians accepted the Bible as the Word of God in the literal sense of verbal inspiration—that every statement in it could be taken as having the direct authority of God. In view of the obviously contradictory statements, records and ideas which the Bible contains, this literal view seems incredible, and must be attributed to a deep-seated need for something definite, unalterable and authoritative to fall back upon, but it has clearly exercised a profound effect on Christian thinking down the ages. It has also, in my view, done a great deal of harm.

It has been harmful because it is basically dishonest, and inculcates a habit of intellectual dishonesty which is all too easy to fall into without the encouragement of dogma. We all tend to rationalize objective facts to fit our own preconceived ideas, but to accept the contradictory statements and records of the Bible as the Word of God, and therefore of guaranteed authority, is to exalt faith—in the dogmatic sense—above truth. In practice, though our minds are often quite capable of accepting contradictory ideas at one and the same time, the usual tendency is to accept a fairly logical system of belief based on selected authorities in the Bible, and to 'interpret' other authorities to make them fit in. All too often, this takes the form of interpreting the teaching of Jesus to reconcile it with Old Testament teaching or with that of St. Paul. Let it be said again that this kind of rationalization is a normal human tendency—we are not nearly as reasonable as we sometimes like to think—but unfortunately in the Christian churches through the ages it has been exaggerated and entrenched as a result of the doctrine of the verbal inspiration of Holy Scripture.

Now, in this modern age, the 'fundamentalist' idea of verbal inspiration is not normally accepted by Protestants though it is not often frankly repudiated either, and we still have habits of mind which are a hangover from that doctrine. From sheer habit of reading the Bible and hearing it read, without facing the implications of its diversity, I find it almost impossible, in spite of all I have said, to think of the great 'I ams' of the fourth Gospel as anything other than the words of Jesus Himself. Many Christians, though they have rejected the idea of the detailed, verbal infallibility of everything in the Bible, still have at the back of their minds a firmly rooted presumption that the Bible—or at least the New Testament—speaks with one voice: authoritative, unified and having the sanctity of 'Holy Writ'. This is an unexamined presumption rather than a clearly stated doctrine, but it still leads to the same tendency to base our system of beliefs on selected Biblical authorities, while avoiding any reference to divergent ideas in the Bible, or—if we cannot avoid them—'interpreting' them to fit in with the particular selection which is congenial to us or to which we have been conditioned by upbringing.

Because the Bible includes so many divergent and often contradictory views, widely differing systems of religious thought can be and have been constructed, all based on the authority of scripture—but on different selections therefrom. The presumption of Biblical unity is so deep-seated that these differing selections can be made quite sincerely and without consciously selecting, and can all be labelled 'Christian' even though parts of them may have no basis in the teaching of Christ. This is surely one reason for the doctrinal divisions of Christendom, and it is the plea of this book that all such systems should be re-examined in the light of the teaching of the Master, who is our primary authority. In the words of the Christian Enquiry Bureau (Free Church) leaflets:

'Christ's life and teaching defines Christianity: He is the standard; His is the all-important central place in the Christian religion, and He is its supreme authority, simply because He has above all others the right to be believed on what Christianity is.' (Leaflet No. 8, p.6)

4 The Dangers of Dogma

> Whosoever will be saved: before all things it is necessary that he hold the Catholick Faith. . . . And the Catholick Faith is this: . . .
>
> Creed of St Athanasius.

EVERY science has its theories. Indeed, no system of study can really be called a science unless it has theories, without which it becomes a mere record of more or less disconnected facts. Ideally, a theory is based on experience. It provides logical connexions between known facts of experience, helps to explain them and also helps to lead beyond experience to further truth. Some theories stay reasonably close to generally accepted facts, while others go far beyond experience and become correspondingly hypothetical and unverifiable.

Similarly, every religion has its doctrines, which in the usual sense of the word are analogous to the theories of science. Ideally, doctrines are based on experience. They provide logical connexions between established facts of experience, help to explain them, and also help to lead beyond experience into new regions of truth. Some doctrines stay reasonably closely to generally accepted facts of experience, while others go far beyond experience and become correspondingly hypothetical and unverifiable.

The analogy between scientific theories and religious doctrines, in this sense, is fairly close, but one important difference lies in the attitude to change. Scientific theories are frequently changing, though some of the basic ones last a long time. As new facts are discovered, old theories from time to time have to be modified, extended or even scrapped and replaced by new ones. Although scientists sometimes cling to old theories with considerable obstinacy, sooner or later they have to give way in the face of new facts. To change or replace out-dated theories is regarded as an advance rather than a retreat.

In religion, doctrines are not nearly so easily changed. This is partly because religious faith is usually based upon events which took place at a given time and cannot in that sense be repeated. In the case of Christianity, the most important 'facts of experience' upon which Christian doctrines rest are the life, teaching, death and resurrection of Jesus. The Christian churches believe that God revealed Himself uniquely and for all time in Jesus, and that belief clearly precludes fundamental changes in some of the doctrines which express it, though there may be wide variations in interpretation.

Doctrines are often expressed in metaphorical or pictorial terms. Even some scientific theories are expressed in pictorial terms in an effort to convey to ordinary minds truths which they otherwise could not grasp. For example, we picture atoms as little balls, and represent molecules by models of balls held together by sticks or springs. We know perfectly well that they are not really like this, but the picture enables us to grasp something of the truth. Similarly doctrines may attempt to explain a 'mystery' in a metaphor —an image intended to convey to our finite minds spiritual truth which we could not otherwise comprehend. A simple example of this is Paul's image of the Church as the 'body of Christ'—a phrase which is so obviously metaphorical that no one is likely to misunderstand it. The danger arises when the picture or metaphor is expressed in a form of words which then becomes established as a dogma—something laid down to be believed by all the faithful.

It is easy to see how the need for dogma must have arisen. As the Christian Church grew and the vivid memory and inspiration of Jesus receded into the past, so people would develop different interpretations of the meaning of the gospel, ideas would be imported from other religions, and in some cases imported beliefs would give rise to pagan practices out of keeping with the teaching of Jesus. It became necessary to set down authoritative statements of the faith, including the basic facts of Jesus and his resurrection, and the fundamental teaching of the apostles about Him. To ensure that all Christians knew these facts and accepted these teachings, the authoritative statements were handed down as dogmas or creeds—to be learned, where appropriate, by heart. The advantages of such authoritative definitions of the faith are obvious, and without them there is no telling what wild ideas would have infected, divided and perhaps destroyed the Church. On the other side, however, there are serious dangers.

The first danger of dogma is that the repetition of a form of words is no substitute for faith. If a dogma explains a spiritual truth in such a way as to help our understanding of it, then it may well be a means of true faith. If, however, it becomes a statement which is imposed as a duty upon Christians it may not have this effect at all. To accept a form of words from a catechism or a creed does not mean that we really believe it even though we may eventually 'believe' by sheer repetition. To repeat a form of words in which we do not fully believe, or about which we have serious mental reservations, introduces an element of dishonesty which could in due course make the whole exercise a sham. How many people, repeating the Apostles' Creed, have doubts about the virgin birth, or the resurrection of the body?—or how many clergy ordained into the Church of England officially accept the Thirty-nine Articles but have mental reservations—to say the least—about the statements on original sin, predestination or the sinfulness of works done before justification? Dogma can easily encourage intellectual dishonesty.

A second danger of dogma is that words can change their meaning, and a dogma which was originally a meaningful explanation of spiritual truth may in due course become misleading or useless. Thus in the doctrine of the

Trinity the English word 'person' is derived from the Latin persona—a player's mask, and one dictionary definition of the word is still a 'character represented, as on a stage'. The Latin version of the doctrine could therefore be thought of as God in three 'characters', or playing three different parts—made known to us in three different ways. But in modern parlance the word 'person' has almost completely lost that meaning, and signifies a separate and independent being, able to make independent decisions. Thus in terms of present day language to speak of 'God in three persons' has become either polytheistic or meaningless. Many people, even some inside the churches, knowing only this modern meaning of the word 'person', must surely hear or repeat the form of words without knowing what on earth it is supposed to mean.

A third disadvantage of dogma is that mental attitudes and thought forms also change with the years, and a mode of expression appropriate to one generation may not be appropriate to another. Thus, 'He descended into Hell' and 'He ascended into Heaven and sitteth on the right hand of God the Father' conveys the idea that Hell is a place in the geographical sense, somewhere under the earth, while Heaven is another place up in the sky where God sits on a throne, somewhere out of sight. This may have conveyed the appropriate spiritual meaning at the time the creed was formulated, but to a normal person in this present generation, not conditioned to the use of these images, it makes the whole thing seem silly. In the absence of established dogma, images or metaphors could be changed to convey truth in the best way to succeeding generations, but the unalterableness of dogma makes this difficult if not impossible, and obstructs rather than encourages a proper understanding of the truth it is supposed to convey.

Finally, dogma tends to inculcate the notion that salvation depends on believing in a certain system of theology or set of statements. This is specifically emphasized, for example, in the Athanasian Creed, prescribed in the English

Prayer Book to be used at Morning Prayer on a number of important feast days. Here are some extracts:

'Whosoever will be saved: before all things it is necessary that he hold the Catholick Faith. Which faith except everyone do keep whole and undefiled: without doubt he shall perish everlastingly. And the Catholick Faith is this: that we worship one God in Trinity, and Trinity in Unity; . . .' (Then follows a long explanation of the meaning of the Trinity.)

'He therefore that it will be saved: must thus think of the Trinity. Furthermore, it is necessary to everlasting salvation: that he also believe rightly the Incarnation of our Lord Jesus Christ.' (Then follows an explanation of the incarnation and person of Christ) . . .

'This is the Catholick Faith: which except a man believe faithfully, he cannot be saved.'

I know of no foundation in the New Testament for the notion that belief in a certain interpretation of the Trinity and of the incarnation of Christ is necessary to salvation—still less that it is 'before all things necessary'.

This last objection to dogma seems to me to be the most serious. Dogma, in the sense of formulated doctrines laid down for 'compulsory' belief, is quite foreign to the teaching of Jesus. According to the synoptic Gospels He taught with a wealth of illustration and metaphor, but also with a considerable freedom of interpretation. His central theme was the kingdom of God and He used many metaphors and similes to explain its nature and meaning. But He did not lay down any dogma about it. According to the fourth Gospel He explained at great length his own relationship with God—and the Athanasian Creed was no doubt founded upon this—but even here it was by way of explanation, not as a formula for compulsory belief.

In short, any attempt to translate a mystery into a formula, to enshrine a spiritual truth in a form of words, carries certain risks. To give such a form of words the authority of an edict laid down for all the faithful is contrary to the spirit of Christ's teaching. This is bad enough when it concerns only the few basic doctrines laid down in the creeds, but it is worse when dogmas are multiplied and elaborated as they have been, for example, in the Roman Catholic Church. The focus on dogma has been, in my view, a second most grievous error of the churches.

5 The Formula for Salvation

'Good Master, what must I do to win eternal life?'
Mark 10: 17

WHEN I wish to travel to London I book my ticket at the station and pay the fare, and thereafter British Rail is under contract to take me all the way. The duties of both parties are clearly defined: on my arrival at Euston neither is in debt to the other and the matter is closed.

From time immemorial there have been those who wanted to have their relationship with God, or the gods, tied up in a nice neat parcel like that—a comfortable, definable, dischargeable transaction. This is what I call 'ticket to heaven' religion. In its crudest forms it may represent popular misconceptions rather than official teaching, but it has been encouraged by many of the metaphors, symbols and rituals through which official teachings are expressed.

The 'ticket' may be a system of sacrifice or ritual observance, or adherence to a code of behaviour; more spiritually, it may be belief in a certain set of doctrines; or it may be simply 'faith'.

A sacrifice in ancient religion was a symbolic payment by which man sought to discharge his obligation to God, hoping thereby to be received into the favour of his deity. The Old Testament tells how the great prophets condemned such sacrificial ritual, but it went on. They failed to break through traditional habits of thinking, or the vested interest of the priests, and the sacrificial system still survived at the time of Christ. A complex routine of public offerings was laid down, with special ones for special occasions, and various forms of private offering for use at times of personal guilt or crisis. No doubt many different ideas lay behind the system, but the dominant theme in the public mind was surely one of propitiation—making things right with God by giving Him presents. As far as the private individual was concerned the presents were paid for, as required, in cash.

The sacrificial system was only part of the business of fulfilling the ritual of the law. Many other observances were required and we gather that the Pharisees maintained a high standard of ritual holiness in their efforts to deserve God's favour. Their 'ticket to heaven' was a difficult one to achieve, but one has the impression from the Gospels that, having once fulfilled their side of the bargain, they were confident that God was under contract to fulfil His.

Jesus drove a coach and horses through the ritual requirements of the law by proclaiming a relationship with God which rested on an entirely different basis. The new wine of His gospel was too explosive for the old wineskins of traditional restrictive authority, and He seemed deliberately to challenge this authority at selected, strategic points. In Mark 2 and 3 there are five instances of this clash between the new gospel and the old authority, concerned with forgiveness, friendship with sinners, fasting and sabbath observance. To the horror of the lawyers he broke the sin barrier by making friends with people normally considered outside the pale of decent society, and by Himself offering forgiveness which was free—that is, not dependent on appropriate observances of the law. To the horror of the Pharisees He broke through the barrier of ritual holiness which was held to be essential for salvation.

At the heart of this challenge was His message that we should think of God as Father, and our relationship with Him should not be one of law, but of love. In a family relationship at its best there is no contract, no balancing of books, no measuring of the duties of one party against those of the other. Of course there are duties and obligations, sometimes very heavy or difficult ones, but they can only be expressed in personal terms, not defined in terms of bargain or law, nor discharged by any method laid down in advance. Of course we can improve the relationship by doing the right things, or break it by doing the wrong things, but there is no point at which either party can say 'I have done what is required of me'.

One reason for the sense of balancing books which still creeps into our theological thinking is that a good deal of Biblical teaching on the subject, other than that of Jesus, was couched in legal or commercial terms. We think of the Old Testament as a bargain—a contract between God and His people. Hebrew religion was centred on the Law. Paul had a legal mind and sometimes expressed his ideas in legal metaphor. Many of the words which still dominate Christian doctrines of the kind we have been discussing draw their meaning from the law courts or otherwise express the sense of contract, or paying a debt, or making good: justification, propitiation, redemption and (in its present day meaning) atonement; and this in spite of the Pauline theme that the Christian is no longer under law but under grace.

In contrast to this, Jesus tended to illustrate His teaching on such matters in more personal terms, such as forgiveness, family relationships, a widow seeking a coin, a shepherd seeking a sheep. When He did use commercial or legal analogies he often did so in such a way as to throw accepted bargain relationships out of joint: for example, the parable of the talents—'The man who has will always be given more . . .'; or of the unjust judge—'This widow is so great a nuisance that I will see her right before she wears me out with her persistence'; or of the labourers in the vineyard—' "Surely I am free to do what I like with my own money. Why be jealous because I am kind?" Thus will the last be first and the first last.'

In a relationship of love there is no measuring, no counting, no balancing, but a perpetual and unmeasured benefit and a perpetual and unmeasured obligation.

This applies equally to the kind of love which Jesus

enjoined for human relationships. In atomic physics there is an 'uncertainty principle' which states, among other things, that it is impossible to define simultaneously both the position and the velocity of an atomic particle. This is not because of any shortcomings in the available methods of measurement but because, according to modern theory, there is at the heart of all matter an inherent degree of indefinableness. At the heart of Christ's teaching about relationships—with God or with other people—there is an analogous principle: a sense in which it is forbidden to specify or measure, because measurement is a denial of the nature of love. When Peter asked what seemed a reasonable question about forgiving his brother and Jesus replied 'Not seven times but seventy times seven', the lesson was surely not that Peter was insufficiently generous, but that he ought not to count. Peter wanted a specification and Jesus refused to give one.

In the same way, in His teaching about man's relationship with God, Jesus illustrated but did not specify. One danger of any formula for salvation, however carefully worded, is that it seeks to provide a specification for something which is in principle unspecifiable. When the rich young man asked the straight question: 'What must I do to win eternal life?'—or, as Matthew's account has it, 'What good must I do to gain eternal life?'—he seemed to be seeking a single kind of action which could be regarded as the key to a right relationship with God, or the essential qualification for eternal life. Jesus' answer, like His reply to the lawyer who asked the same question on another occasion, seemed unsatisfactory. In effect He said to both enquirers: keep the commandments and do good to others—a reply broadly in keeping with the message of the prophets so eloquently summed up in Micah 6: 8: 'What does the Lord require of you but to do justice and to love kindness, and to walk humbly with your God.' But He did not give them the answer they seemed to be seeking. He was asked for a specification and He declined to specify.

In the fourth Gospel, of course, the message is quite different, for here the key word is faith—faith in Christ: 'Everyone who looks upon the Son and puts his faith in him shall possess eternal life.' This sounds very much like a ticket to heaven if taken literally, but it is rash to take the fourth Gospel too literally.

Unfortunately the notion of a ticket to heaven dies hard, and has survived in various forms in the churches in spite of the teaching of Jesus. It tends to arise whenever there is emphasis on priests and sacrifices, and whenever there is emphasis on a formula for salvation.

It is one of the remarkable things about the early Christians that from the beginning they had no priests and no sacrifices. A priest is someone who officiates at a sacrifice and in other ways mediates between God and man. For the early Christians, still conscious of the presence of the risen Christ, there was no need of priests; and Jesus plainly taught that sacrifices were not necessary for the purpose of obtaining God's favour. Nevertheless, the absence of priests and sacrifices in the early Church was a truly revolutionary break for people brought up in the Hebrew tradition. In one sense they seem to have rationalized it to themselves by thinking of Christ as their new and only High Priest, and by regarding His death on the Cross as the 'one perfect and sufficient sacrifice for the sins of the whole world'; while in another sense, perhaps, they sublimated the idea by dedicating themselves as 'living sacrifices'. Whatever the explanation, it is plain from the New Testament that the faith and practice of the early Christians was entirely non-sacerdotal.

Somewhere in the Church's later history the institution of priesthood became established again and the communion meal, which St. Paul called 'the Lord's Supper' and St. Luke 'the breaking of bread', came to be regarded as a sacrifice—a re-presentation of the sacrifice of Christ—at which only a priest could officiate. This appears to be the established thinking of the Roman Catholic Church today.

To quote from leaflet No. 11 of the Catholic Enquiry Centre's course on the Catholic Faith:

'The Mass is called a sacrifice. A sacrifice is an offering... It is an offering which is only given to God. And it is an offering made by a person specially appointed to make it —a priest.'

It is explained that the purpose of this gift is partly to thank God for all He has given and partly to make reparation for sins, and in the previous leaflet it is emphasized that the Mass is the central point of the Catholic religion.

It is not possible to reconcile this view of the Mass, as the Christian's central means of receiving God's blessing, with the simple, non-ritual teaching of Jesus about forgiveness, prayer and entering the kingdom of God. To interpose into the child-Father relationship which he taught the need for a specially administered gift or sacrifice—however symbolically we may think of that term—is contrary to the whole trend of His teaching.

The same faith in the efficacy of observances as such is apparent in some other practices, notably in the case of infant baptism because here the child can play no conscious part in the proceedings. To quote again from the 21 lessons in the Catholic Faith:

'Washing with water is a perfectly ordinary thing. It cleanses stains. Our Lord takes that ordinary thing and says, in effect, when you wash with water in the name of the Father and of the Son and of the Holy Ghost then that washing becomes a supernatural thing. It washes away the stain of original sin.'

I know of nothing Jesus said which could justify that statement, and when the reasoning is applied to infant baptism it is not unduly cynical to describe the operation as 'magic'.

Another and quite different kind of 'ticket to heaven' consists in purchasing salvation, not by sacrifices or observances, but by belief in doctrines. The 'Athanasian' Creed already referred to, with its categorical statement that belief in a certain interpretation of the Trinity and the Incarnation is before all things necessary to salvation, and that those who do not so believe cannot be saved, is about as near a ticket to heaven as you could get.

This may not have been quite the intention of the framers of the creed, but it has almost certainly represented the belief of many in both Catholic and Protestant churches—for example, at times when Protestants or Catholics have thought it necessary to burn at the stake those who professed the other faith. No doubt there were many motives behind such actions, some less worthy than others, but to the extent that they were sincere they surely sprang from the basic notion that the fate of a man's immortal soul depended above all upon whether he gave his allegiance to the right or the wrong set of religious beliefs. To us in this day and age it seems incredible that men who had studied the teachings of Jesus should be guilty of doing such acts in His name, but the idea behind it is not yet dead. The Athanasian Creed may not now be taken very seriously by Anglicans, but it is still officially part of that church's doctrine and officially supposed to be read on specified occasions.

A different formula for salvation which can smack very strongly of the ticket-to-heaven idea arises directly out of St. Paul's doctrine of justification by faith and the fourth Gospel's version of Jesus's teaching: 'Everyone who looks upon the Son and puts his faith in him shall possess eternal life.'

This theme will be dealt with separately in the next chapter. The purpose of the present reference is to note that it has often been, and sometimes still is, expressed as a categorical formula, an exclusive principle or specification for salvation, brooking no exceptions and no alternative explanations of the truth. Thus John Wesley, in the first of his standard 44 Sermons—of which the title, 'Salvation by Faith', is a subtle misquotation from Scripture—says: 'Wherewithal, then, shall a sinful man atone for any the least of his sins? With his own works? No. Were they ever so many or holy, they are not his own, but God's . . .'. The word 'atone' clearly signifies payment or compensation. Faith, to use the Pauline phrase, is counted for righteousness and sinful man, having nothing wherewith to pay for his ticket, is provided with a free one.

It is still often stated, as a characteristic belief of the evangelical churches, that 'we are saved by faith alone'. The little word 'alone' is a non-Biblical addition and has the effect of making this statement more categorical, more of a formula, than the Biblical passages from which it is derived.

It might be thought that Wesley's 'black or white' interpretation of this theme is no longer taken seriously, but this unfortunately is far from true. In Chapter 1 we referred to the 1963 Report of the Conversations between the Church of England and the Methodist Church. After this Report had been approved in principle by the Methodist Conference, a statement was issued by the four Methodist members of the original Commission who had dissented from the Report. Its purpose was to clarify their position in the light of developments and in it they expressed their point of view by referring to five authoritative quotations. None of the quotations, one need hardly say, made any reference to the teaching of Christ—any more than the original Report had done, but the fifth, quoted with emphasis and approval, was from Wesley's Sermon 5: 'Faith is the *necessary* condition of justification; yea, and the *only necessary* condition thereof.' Nothing could be more categorical and exclusive than that.

Finally, let us take a look at what might be called the classical Christian doctrine of man, sin and salvation, covering the whole gamut of Biblical theology. It runs something like this:

God created man perfect and without sin, but with freedom to choose either obedience and life, or disobedience and death.

Man, in the person of Adam, chose disobedience and

thus sin and death came into the world.

All men after Adam, inheriting Adam's sin, are deserving of death, and of themselves can do nothing to redeem their fallen state.

In the fullness of time God in His mercy sent His Son into the world to redeem fallen mankind. Christ, though Himself sinless, died for our sins and by His death satisfied the eternal justice of God, the obedience of Christ cancelling the disobedience of Adam.

Through His sacrifice man could once more be reconciled to God and be counted worthy of eternal life, Christ having offered the 'one perfect and sufficient sacrifice for the sins of the whole world'.

How much of this do we believe? There are some who still firmly believe the whole lot, or say they do. But many more of us have pushed these ideas to the back of our minds, like a skeleton in the cupboard, and are reluctant to take them out and look at them for fear the whole structure falls to pieces. We retain them in a mental twilight, half believing, half disbelieving them and not having the courage either to accept or reject.

The first difficulty assailing this classical system was the rise of scientific theories of evolution, now broadly accepted by all thinking people, according to which we think of man as a product of development from lower forms of life. In this context Adam becomes a sort of symbolic representative of the human race and 'the fall' has to be linked somehow with the basic animal passions which we inherit from our animal ancestors. But, quite apart from this difficulty, the whole system seems to be a synthesis of several different themes, some based on primitive ideas of sacrifice and scapegoats, others on much later conceptions of the nature and character of God; and the different themes cannot be reconciled with one another.

Thus, is it reasonable or just to say that because Adam sinned, all subsequent generations of men are guilty?—unfortunate, perhaps, but surely not guilty or deserving of punishment? Or again, if God is merciful, how could He possibly inflict eternal punishment on men for sins which they were by nature incapable of avoiding? And if God's eternal justice somehow requires that punishment should be meted out for sin, how could it possibly be 'just' to accept the sufferings of a sinless one in payment of the debt?—'There was no other good enough to pay the price of sin'.

People in different ages think in different terms, and this system of thought, which for earlier generations may have been an adequate expression of sincere Christian faith, has in terms of present day patterns of thought become at best contradictory and confusing, and at worst positively blasphemous, by imputing to God—however symbolically—the kind of actions and motives which in a human being we should regard as vicious and unjust.

We all find it difficult to shake off the shackles of dogma once they have been established, and there is a natural hesitation to face up to the inconsistencies of traditional Christian thinking—partly because we are conditioned to accept it and do not notice the inconsistencies, partly because of our unwillingness to offend sincere Christians and divide the Church still further. But the time has surely come to lay aside these formulas and systems of thought which have become crystallized over the years, and to start all over again, beginning—if we still profess to be Christians—with the teaching of Christ Himself.

6 The Evangelical Divergence

THE evangelical divergence takes the form of selecting certain Pauline themes which already differ in emphasis from the teaching of Christ; modifying them in such a way as to widen that difference; and then pronouncing them to be key doctrines of the faith.

Paul's letters were written to meet the needs of particular people and particular situations. The 'faith—not works' theme sprang out of his own vivid experience of Christ and was a counterblast to the judaizing tendencies of some Jewish Christians who wanted to tie the new faith to the old observances of the Law. At times when this theme has been especially revived—for example by Luther and Wesley—there may have been again a particular need for that particular emphasis. But those who make the theme a key doctrine of general application, rather than a special emphasis to meet a particular need, do so at the cost of ignoring much of the teaching of Jesus. This applies particularly to the Methodist Church.

The Methodist Local Preachers' Department in 1951 issued a booklet on 'Doctrinal Preaching', specially prepared by a committee of experts for the guidance of lay preachers, and with particular emphasis on 'our doctrines'—that is, the characteristic theological emphases of Methodism. After dealing with the urgency of doctrinal preaching and the Biblical basis of that preaching, the authors devoted a whole chapter to the gospel as preached by the apostles, with a long appendix on the gospel as preached by St. Paul; this was followed by a chapter on 'Our Doctrines'. There was nothing, not even a single sentence, about the gospel as preached by Christ.

Characteristically, the booklet contained 51 references to

Paul's letters compared with 8 references to passages from the four Gospels. Only one of these eight (Luke 16: 15) had any connection with the themes discussed under 'Our Doctrines', and even that was an indirect one. In explaining the characteristic doctrines of the Methodist Church they made no reference at all, either directly or indirectly, to the teaching of Christ. The last chapter consisted of an outline sermon on the theme which they evidently considered the most important, 'Justification by Faith', and about this they said: 'It was not in vain that this doctrine became the corner stone of Protestant doctrine at the Reformation, and that John Wesley acclaimed it as fundamental Christian doctrine.'

The twin ideas of 'salvation by faith' and 'justification by faith' are difficult to disentangle from one another because they are really derived from two different Biblical expressions of the same central theme; that God's grace is free to all who will receive it in faith, and we cannot by our own efforts either achieve or deserve it. For the purpose of comparison with the teaching of Christ, however, we will try to deal with the two ideas separately.

Salvation by faith is in close accord with the theme of the fourth Gospel. It is emphatically not in accord with the teaching recorded in Matthew, Mark and Luke.

In the synoptic Gospels there are a few incidents involving individuals for whom 'faith', broadly interpreted, could be considered the key to salvation; for example, Jesus said to the woman who anointed his feet: 'Your faith has saved you', and to Zacchaeus on his declaration of repentance: 'Salvation has come to this house today!' On the other hand, in his explicit teaching about entering the kingdom of God, or eternal life, Jesus did not mention faith. He did mention quite a number of necessary qualifications, some with great emphasis: repentance, childlikeness, goodness, keeping the commandments, self-denial, helpfulness to others, and hearing His words and acting on them. Some of these undoubtedly come into the category of 'works' rather than faith, and the salient points of this teaching could be summarized thus: if you want to qualify for the kingdom of God, keep the commandments and do good to others. This is in direct contrast to the evangelical doctrine of salvation by faith alone.

Turning now to the second doctrine, the word 'justification', according to Wesley, means 'pardon and acceptance with God'. Jesus had little to say about justification as such, though He did use the word in the parable of the Pharisee and the Publican; in this illustration the taxgatherer was 'justified' because he admitted his guilt and asked for pardon.

On the other hand, Jesus had much to say about forgiveness, both directly and by implication. In the parable of the Prodigal Son, for example, the younger son received pardon and acceptance only after he had done two things:

1. repented, and
2. actively turned away from his evil life.

Neither of these can be described by the word 'faith'. In the Lord's Prayer Jesus linked God's forgiveness with our willingness to forgive others and emphasized the link with the parable of the unforgiving servant. In another saying He enjoined anyone who had a gift for the altar to go back and be reconciled with his brother *before* offering the gift.

Characteristically, Jesus did not give any single formula for receiving pardon and acceptance with God, but the conditions which He thought it necessary to emphasize were repentance and willingness to forgive others. The one approach which He emphasized more than others seems to have been: to be right with God, you must first be right with other people. Wesley's categorical statement that faith is 'the *only necessary* condition' of justification is therefore a blatant denial of Christ's teaching.

If we take Christ's teaching as the standard, then the evangelical divergence seems to me to rest on two basic errors, both very important.

The first error is that it debases the nature of man; it attributes to ordinary people a fundamentally lower nature than Jesus did. The booklet on doctrinal preaching referred to above expressed it thus: the Christian doctrine of man 'begins with the blunt and uncompromising statement that man is a sinner, and it drives the statement home with disconcerting directness'. Jesus did not begin there. Of course man is far from perfect. Of course 'all have sinned, all come short of the glory of God'. But to accept that self-evident truth is poles apart from the statement that the central fact of man's nature, and the starting point for Christian thinking in the matter, is that he is a sinner.

This view of man is closely linked with the classical doctrine of the Fall, according to which God made man perfect and without sin, but Satan intervened and spoiled it all. It was therefore, so to speak, not God's fault that man became a sinner, since He had originally done His work well. If we do not accept this primitive picture of the Fall, then it is a gross insult to our Creator to dismiss man contemptuously as 'a sinner'.

It is characteristic of the childlike simplicity of mythology that the classical doctrine of man saw the Fall as a transition from completely good to completely bad. John Wesley apparently accepted this and drove the point home with his usual clarity. Continuing the passage already quoted from his Sermon 1 on 'Salvation by Faith': 'But indeed they' (the works of man) 'are all unholy and sinful themselves, so that every one of them needs a fresh atonement. Only corrupt fruit grows on a corrupt tree. And his heart is altogether corrupt and abominable; being "come short of the glory of God", the glorious righteousness at first impressed on his soul, after the image of his great Creator. Therefore, having nothing, neither righteousness nor works, to plead, his mouth is utterly stopped before God.'

In another sermon he drew the same all-or-nothing distinction between the converted and the unconverted, by an emphatically literal interpretation of John's 'He that is born of God doth not commit sin'. He thus divided people, against all experience, into two categories—the unregenerate, who are completely bad, and the 'born again', who are completely good.

This view of man finds no echo in the teaching and actions of Christ, whose approach was much nearer to the modern, common-sense view. An intelligent observer of today, accepting the evolutionary explanation that man has evolved over millions of years from lower animals, will be conscious that many of our sins derive directly from inherited animal instincts, while others represent the misuse of those powers and insights which distinguish us from other animals. Against this background the essential characteristic of man is his potential goodness: that he is capable of aesthetic appreciations, moral decisions and spiritual insights which, within the limits of our knowledge, are not to be found anywhere else in God's creation. Looking round at people and events as they are, our intelligent observer, unfettered by 'Christian' dogmas, will see that there is that of God in every man, pagan or Christian, converted or unconverted; that everyone has some good in him but no one is perfect; and that people differ in the degree of good or evil in their lives.

Jesus' approach was quite close to that, though His measures of good and evil differed from contemporary standards. He saw much evil in people normally classified as good and much good in people normally classified as 'sinners'. In His stories about people and His dealings with people, He recognized and commended the good actions of many who were 'unconverted', without the slightest suggestion that all their actions were 'unholy and sinful in themselves'. It would be nearer to His attitude to say, not that man is a sinner, but that men and women are potential saints. There is a world of difference between the two.

Another aspect of this debasement of the nature of man is the idea that we can do nothing of ourselves to help our 'fallen' state. Again it smacks of the all-or-nothing habit so dear to classical theologians and their modern apologists. Anxious to repudiate the humanistic view that man can look after himself without any help from God, they plunge into the opposite extreme that man can do nothing at all. As a piece of rhetorical humility this may be harmless, but as a serious statement of doctrine it is unrelated to real people and completely at variance with the teaching and actions of Jesus. Real people, be they never so evangelically minded, behave as if they were to be held responsible for their actions, including—or especially—their good ones. And Jesus treated people in that light, as persons having in themselves the ability to make moral decisions, not as automata waiting for God to switch them on and feed into them the necessary instructions.

John Wesley pursued the *reductio ad absurdum* to the bitter end by saying that even the faith by which we receive salvation is not our own, but the gift of God—an idea derived from Ephesians 2: 8, which in the New English Bible is given quite a different slant. In one sense this is begging the question because, as part of God's creation, all that we have and are is a gift from Him and we live and move and have our being in Him; but if it has any meaning that makes it worth saying, it downgrades men and women to something less than persons. Jesus did the opposite. He emphasized each man's responsibility for his good or bad actions, commending the good and condemning the bad. With the exception of the notorious few who had a high opinion of themselves, he lifted people up by his estimation of them, exalting human nature and human personality.

The second basic error of the evangelical divergence is that it makes a right relationship with God self-dependent, whereas Christ made it dependent on a right relationship with others. Perhaps we may illustrate this with the analogy of 'vertical' and 'horizontal' which has often been used.

To erect a pole it is usual to attach at least three ropes or wires to the top. These are used both to draw it up to the vertical position and also to maintain it there once raised.

It is held safely vertical only as long as it is firmly linked with widely spaced positions on the horizontal level. The vertical relationship depends upon the horizontal.

The great Old Testament prophets denounced religious observances which were independent of right human relationships. The sacrifices, new moons, sabbath observances, solemn assemblies and so on which they condemned were 'vertical' transactions—dealings between man and God. The attitude which they condemned was the one which made these the central feature of religion, and their message was, in effect: God does not want you to give gifts to Him; He wants you to do good to other people.

Jesus taught the same message in His own characteristic way. God's forgiveness depends upon our forgiveness of others, and in the New English Bible this dependence is emphasized by the use of the past tense: 'Forgive us the wrong we have done, as we have forgiven those who have wronged us'. And again: 'First go and make peace with your brother, and only then come back and offer your gift'. Or again: 'I tell you this, anything you did for one of my brothers here, however humble, you did for me.' A right relationship with God begins with, and continues in, a right relationship with other people.

The essence of the evangelical divergence is its categorical assertion that justification, or salvation, depends only on faith—something entirely between ourselves and God. It asserts that nothing we can do is significant and acceptance with God requires only that we put our faith in Him; that being right with God comes first, and being right with other people only follows from it. This is the reverse of what Jesus taught.

7 From Metaphor to Metaphysics

'Hypotheses should not be multiplied without necessity.'
William of Occam

A SIMILE is an expression which illustrates the nature of one thing by comparing it with another.

According to the Gospels of Matthew and Luke, Jesus used many telling similes to illustrate his teaching and particularly to explain what he meant by the kingdom of God, or the kingdom of Heaven. Here is a selection:

I send you out like sheep among wolves.

How shall I describe this generation? They are like children sitting in the market place . . .

Alas for you, lawyers and Pharisees, hypocrites! You are like tombs covered with whitewash.

The kingdom of Heaven is like mustard seed, which a man took and sowed in his field.

,, ,, ,, ,, is like yeast, which a woman took and mixed with half a hundredweight of flour.

,, ,, ,, ,, is like treasure lying buried in a field.

,, ,, ,, ,, is like a net let down into the sea.

,, ,, ,, ,, is like this. A man sowed his field with good seed.

,, ,, ,, ,, is like this. There was once a landowner . . .

,, ,, ,, ,, is like this. There was a king who prepared a feast . .

Though the comparisons are somewhat bewildering in their variety, each one drives home its own aspect of truth. There is not much danger of misunderstanding the meaning, or of reading into the similes more than they were obviously intended to convey. No one, for example, is likely to conclude that the kingdom of heaven is a small, round, solid object, or an open mesh made of string. We do not dream of taking the similes of Jesus 'literally'.

A metaphor is an implied simile—one from which the word 'like' has been omitted. Because of this omission a metaphor—intentionally or otherwise—sometimes conveys a more far-reaching meaning than the corresponding simile. For example, 'All we like sheep have gone astray' conveys the strictly limited meaning that we are sheeplike only in our tendency to go astray. On the other hand, 'We are all sheep who have gone astray' conveys the subtle impression that we are fundamentally sheeplike and that going astray is merely one indication of that property. A metaphor, therefore, may bring home a meaning more vividly than a simile, but it may also be less specific and therefore more subject to misunderstanding.

The synoptic Gospels, especially Matthew and Luke, also record many metaphors of Jesus. Indeed, His facility for expressing spiritual truths in terms of vivid simile and metaphor must surely have been part of His effectiveness and popularity as a preacher. Here are some examples:

You are light for all the world.

You are salt to the world.

I have come to set fire to the earth.

I will make you fishers of men.

You are Peter, the Rock; and on this rock I will build my church.

The crop is heavy, but labourers are scarce.

Go and tell that fox . . .

This is what the parable means. The seed is the word of God . . .

You viper's brood!

The fourth Gospel has few similes but abounds in metaphor—with a characteristic 'Johannine' flavour. The seven great 'I ams' we have already mentioned express the nature and work of Christ in terms of dramatic and compelling metaphors, and in some cases the text—such as 'I am the good shepherd' is only the focal point of a discourse which is wholly metaphorical. Other examples of the use of metaphor in the fourth Gospel are:

There is the Lamb of God; it is he who takes away the sin of the world.

Destroy this temple and in three days I will raise it again.

Whoever drinks the water that I shall give him will never suffer thirst any more.

The use of metaphor in the fourth Gospel is frankly acknowledged in Chapter 16: 'Till now I have been using figures of speech; a time is coming when I shall no longer use figures, but tell you of the Father in plain words.'

Another kind of figure of speech used by Jesus in the synoptic Gospels is hyperbole—a dramatic exaggeration which may also be metaphorical, rather similar to the exaggerated figures of speech we often use in ordinary conversation: 'You could have knocked me down with a feather' or 'I'm sick to death of the whole thing'—expressions which are never for one moment intended to be taken literally. The following are some hyperbolic expressions of Jesus:

Why do you look at the speck of sawdust in your brother's eye with never a thought for the great plank in your own?

Blind guides! You strain off a midge, yet gulp down a camel!

If your right eye leads you astray, tear it out and fling it away.

You need only say to this mountain, 'Be lifted from your place and hurled into the sea' and what you say will be done.

It is easier for a camel to pass through the eye of a needle than for a rich man to enter the kingdom of God.

If anyone comes to me and does not hate his father and mother, wife and children, brothers and sisters, even his own life, he cannot be a disciple of mine.

In studying the Gospels it is sometimes difficult to tell when metaphor and hyperbole end and plain words begin. Apparently even the disciples, familiar as they were with the language and idiom of Jesus, sometimes took His metaphor too literally, as when He said 'Beware of the leaven of the Pharisees' and they thought He was talking about bread. There are some passages which were obviously metaphorical and others which were obviously intended to be taken literally, but quite a few in between about which we may be very uncertain. This probably does not matter until we try to imprison the vivid, free-ranging style of Jesus's teaching in the strait-jacket of defined dogma and formula.

Let us consider the words 'son' and 'father'. In their ordinary meaning they signify a biological relationship between human beings. When Jesus said God is our heavenly Father, therefore, he was using the word in a metaphorical sense. Similarly, 'Son of Man' was a metaphorical expression embodying Old Testament ideas of a sort of supreme representative of man before God, while 'Son of God' was another metaphor used in a special sense about Jesus Himself. According to the synoptic Gospels Jesus preferred to refer to Himself as Son of Man, and the contrast between the two metaphors as descriptions of Messiah is brought out clearly in Luke's account of Christ's examination before the Council:

'Tell us,' they said, 'are you the Messiah?'

'If I tell you', he replied, 'you will not believe me; and if I ask questions, you will not answer. But from now on, the Son of Man will be seated at the right hand of Almighty God.'

'You are the Son of God, then?', they all said, and he replied, 'It is you who say I am'.

According to this account Jesus, while still preferring the metaphor 'Son of Man', did not deny the validity of the other metaphor, as much as to say, 'You could call it that if you like, but it is not the expression I would use'.

'Son of God', however, was the expression the author of the fourth Gospel used, and the Church has followed his example. Accepting the story of the virgin birth as given in Matthew and Luke, the Church, while maintaining that we are all children of God in a metaphorical sense, established the view that Jesus was Son of God in a more than metaphorical sense: 'begotten, not created' and 'conceived by the Holy Ghost, born of the Virgin Mary.' What would otherwise be a metaphorical expression intended to convey a difficult meaning by expressing it in familiar terms was thus interpreted as a physical or metaphysical reality.

I do not know at what stage this was adopted by the Church, but it is interesting to note that in the records we have Jesus made no reference to anything special about His own birth; that the apostles in their early preaching also made no reference to it and spoke of Jesus as Messiah rather than Son of God; that Paul in his letter to the Romans (about A.D. 57) used Son of God in the metaphorical sense and apparently knew nothing of the story of the virgin birth:

'This gospel God announced beforehand in sacred scriptures through his prophets. It is about his Son: on the human level he was born of David's stock, but on the level of the spirit—the Holy Spirit—he was declared Son of God by a mighty act in that he rose from the dead.'

Even the writer of the fourth Gospel (A.D. 90-110), who set out specifically to show that Christ is Son of God, did not refer to the virgin birth in support of that view, and clearly stated, as we have seen, that much of the teaching in his record was metaphorical—'Till now I have been using figures of speech . . .'.

It is fairly clear, therefore, without making any judgement on the validity of either interpretation, that the metaphysical as distinct from the metaphorical interpretation of Christ's sonship only became the established thinking of Christians at a fairly late stage.

Of the many and varied metaphors of Jesus, a few have been selected by the Church and given a metaphysical rather than metaphorical interpretation. This applies particularly to Catholic doctrines connected with the Mass. One of the relevant passages in the Catholic Enquiry Centre's leaflets (No. 10) reads:

'Christ takes bread in his hands. He blesses it and breaks it. "Take ye this and eat. This is My Body." And then he takes the Chalice: "Drink ye all of this. This is My Blood of the New Testament which shall be shed for many unto remission of sins." (Matthew 26).

'The Catholic Church teaches that He meant what He said.'

It is emphasized that because Jesus solemnly used the words 'This is My Body. This is My Blood,' the Church therefore holds that 'When the priest repeats those words in obedience to Christ's command: "Do this for a commemoration of Me": what was bread is now no longer bread, what was wine is no longer wine. It is the Body and Blood of Christ.'

There are other metaphors in the Gospels which use the same turn of phrase, for example: 'You are Peter, the Rock. And on this rock will I build my church.' As far as I know, no one suggests that this should be interpreted in any other than a metaphorical sense, or claims that Peter was at that moment transformed by the power of God into a rock, though still retaining all the appearances of a human being. Did Jesus 'mean what he said' when He called Peter a rock?

The Catholic interpretation of 'This is my body' is not only metaphysical in the sense that what has all the physical characteristics of bread and wine is said to be in reality something quite different; but it also involves a transference in time in two senses: in the first place, Jesus actually said 'This is my body' before his death, while his body was still whole, and the Catholic version of Matthew 26: 28 puts the sentence in two tenses: 'This is my blood . . . which shall be shed.' In the second place, His words are said to apply 'literally' not only to the bread and wine he himself distributed but also to all subsequent portions of bread and wine over which a priest has said the appropriate words. Apparently in justification of this second time transference the leaflet quotes from the discourse on the Bread of Life in the fourth Gospel (John 6: 47):

'You can have no life in yourselves unless you eat the Flesh of the Son of Man and drink His Blood . . . My Flesh is real food, My Blood is real drink. He who eats My Flesh and drinks My Blood lives continually in Me and I in him.'

This passage is part of a metaphorical discourse which has several counterparts in the fourth Gospel, expressed in the same kind of terms. There is, for example, the discourse on the Vine in Chapter 15:

'I am the real vine, and my Father is the gardener . . .

'I am the vine, you are the branches. He who dwells in me, as I dwell in him, bears much fruit; for apart from me you can do nothing.'

Assuming for the sake of argument that these were the actual words of Jesus, does anyone suggest that they should be interpreted in any sense other than metaphorical, or that Christ 'meant what He said' when He declared 'I am the real vine'—that He was in fact a vine though retaining all the appearances of a man, and that his disciples were really branches, although in the physical sense they still appeared to be human beings?

Or again, in Chapter 10 there is the metaphorical discourse on the shepherd and the sheep, in which Jesus refers to himself, with solemn emphasis, as a door:

'In truth, in very truth I tell you, I am the door of the sheepfold. The sheep paid no heed to any who came before me, for these were all thieves and robbers. I am the door; anyone who comes into the fold through me shall be safe.'

The metaphors are a little mixed here, but that does not affect the point. Does anyone, in spite of the emphatic 'In truth, in very truth I tell you', suggest that Jesus 'meant what He said'—that He was really a door, while still preserving the appearance of a man? Of course not—like the Vine and the Bread the words are metaphorical.

The Catholic Church, then, has *selected* certain passages from the Gospels—each of them readily capable of interpretation in the metaphorical sense—and has chosen to interpret them metaphysically instead. Protestants, of course, would hold that Christ is present in spirit when Christians worship in sincerity, but His presence in the Catholic Mass is evidently thought of as something more, and is called 'The Real Presence'. Matthew's Gospel reports Jesus as saying 'Where two or three have met together in my name, I am there among them'—without the need for sacrifice, altar or priest. Is this kind of presence 'Real' or not?

I have dwelt at some length on this Catholic doctrine of the 'Real Presence'—although it must surely have been the subject of many far more learned discourses—because it seems to me to illustrate a fundamental attitude which tends to lead away from the teaching of Jesus. In my view the doctrine is an unnecessary metaphysical device:

Metaphysical because it postulates a 'reality' which is

somehow different from what we would call a spiritual truth, yet which is independent of observable physical reality and cannot be related to it;

Device because the relevant words of Jesus as reported in the Gospels cannot in fact be interpreted literally—His body was still alive when He said 'This is my body'—and a special kind of mystery has been created in order to avoid the conclusion that His words were metaphorical;

Unnecessary because I can see no reason why these particular expressions should not be interpreted as metaphor in the same way as many other vivid metaphorical expressions of Jesus.

It is not possible to prove or disprove the truth of a metaphysical interpretation, and it might be justified on the ground that it assists faith, worship and dedication; but according to my reading of the Gospels this approach does not seem to be in keeping with the teaching of Jesus and it carries the serious danger that once metaphysical speculation creeps into religion it can carry people a very long way from both the teaching of the Master and the verifiable facts of experience. A fascinating example of this is provided by the Roman Catholic doctrines about the Blessed Virgin Mary, such as her bodily assumption into heaven.

I will try to summarize the teaching on Mary as outlined in leaflet No. 18 of the course already referred to, while recognizing that one cannot do justice to a brief outline by summarizing it still further. The outline refers for authority to certain Gospel passages, yet the connexion between the conclusions and the scripture passages from which they appear to be derived is so slender that there must surely have been other reasons, not mentioned in the leaflet, in support of the doctrines outlined:

1. The teaching about Mary is central to the Catholic faith, and unless one understands it one cannot understand the Catholic faith.
2. Since Jesus was Himself God, then Mary is called

Mother of God, as was solemnly defined in the Third General Council of the Church in A.D. 431.

3. Because, in Luke's account of the annunciation, the angel called Mary 'full of grace'—the New English Bible translates it 'most favoured one!'—it is concluded that she was entirely without sin—that is, she never committed any personal sin in her life and from the first moment of her existence she was free from any stain of original sin (the 'immaculate conception').
4. From Mary's reply 'How shall this be done, for I know not man?' (N.E.B.: 'I have no husband'), it is concluded not only that Mary was a virgin at the time, but that she remained a virgin for the rest of her life.
5. At the wedding feast in Cana, Jesus changed His mind and turned the water into wine as a result of His mother's persuasion. The significance of this miracle was to show us how powerful are the prayers of His Mother with Jesus.
6. Jesus' words from the Cross: 'Behold, thy mother' are taken to mean that our Lord gave His Mother at this point to be our Mother also.
7. When the term of her natural life was ended, Mary was assumed body and soul into heaven.

The term 'Mother of God', though it may be picturesque and helpful to some, seems an odd expression to be explained in terms of theological belief. If God is creator of all things, how can He have had a mother? And if we prefer to express her special significance in picturesque rather than in more precise theological terms, since she is said to have been the Mother of God's Son, would it not be more appropriate to call her 'Wife of God'? Perhaps this is quibbling over words, but it does emphasize the air of fanciful unreality which surrounds the whole subject.

What seems to me most alarming in the development of

this theme is the series of remarkable non-sequiturs which it contains; if this kind of reasoning is allowed, one can think up almost anything a twisted mind could fancy and by a suitable selection of texts claim that it derives from the teaching of Jesus. To draw from the brief compliment 'full of grace' the conclusion that the recipient never committed any personal sin in her life and had been born entirely free from original sin—whatever that may mean in real terms—displays such breathtaking inventiveness that one throws up one's hands in despair. The same applies to the conclusion that Mary remained a virgin all her life—in spite of obvious Biblical evidence to the contrary—because she is reported to have said 'I know not man'; that the incident at the Cana wedding feast was an indication that Christians twenty centuries later should ask Mary to pray on their behalf; and that Jesus was giving her to be 'our Mother' when He asked the beloved disciple to adopt her as his.

As far as I can see, the only bit of this whole theme which has any basis in the Bible is item 4—and that a very shaky one.

There is nothing in the teaching or actions of Jesus as recorded in the four Gospels to suggest that He regarded His Mother as in any way fundamentally different from other mothers; or that the manner of His birth had any bearing on the gospel; or that He expected His first disciples or future disciples to pay her any special reverence, or to think of her as in any way assisting in their worship or prayer; though one incident, recorded in Matthew and Mark, would appear on the face of it to have the opposite implication (Matthew 12: 46):

'He was still speaking to the crowd when his mother and his brothers appeared; they stood outside, wanting to speak to him. Someone said, "Your mother and your brothers are here outside; they want to speak to you." Jesus turned to the man who brought the message, and said, "Who is my mother? Who are my brothers?"; and pointing to the disciples, he said, "Here are my mother and my brothers. Whoever does the will of my heavenly Father is my brother, my sister, my mother." '

In guiding His disciples in prayer and worship, Jesus taught them repeatedly and consistently, by precept, parable and example, to pray direct to their heavenly Father, without the need for priest or sacrifice and without the mediation of anyone else—except, perhaps, in the fourth Gospel, that of Jesus Himself. The objection to the Mary-centred worship of Catholicism, therefore, is that—however psychologically satisfying it may be to those who are brought up to it—it has no basis at all in the recorded teaching and example of Christ, and is in direct contrast to His emphasis on free and direct communion between a man and his heavenly Father.

It is probable, of course, that the apostles knew and remembered aspects of the teaching of Jesus which are not recorded in the Gospels as we have them; but I know of no reference to the mother of Jesus in the preaching outlined in the Acts of the Apostles, nor in any of the writings of Paul, nor indeed of any other New Testament author. The Virgin Mary cult was obviously and flagrantly added to the Church's teaching at a later stage—probably an idea imported from paganism and modified to fit into the Christian tradition. Indeed, the expression 'Queen of Heaven' which Catholics sometimes use is embarrassingly similar to the title often given by ancient pagan religions to their chief goddess.

One very interesting development of this cult is the doctrine of the bodily assumption of the Blessed Virgin Mary. When we were young we sometimes played a party game called 'Pass it on', in which a short story was told, or a drawing copied, from each to the next one down a line of people. The amusement lay in seeing how frequently the final version of the story or drawing bore no resemblance to the original. I am reminded of this by the process of reasoning outlined in the Catholic leaflets to lead up to the belief in bodily assumption. It is a sort of philosophical game of 'pass it on', a multi-stage metaphysical syllogism which runs something like this:

1. The angel addressed Mary as 'full of grace'.
2. She must therefore have been free from sin.
3. This means that Christ redeemed His mother, from the very first moment of her life, so that she was conceived without any stain of original sin.
4. Death and corruption are the consequence of original sin—'By one man sin entered into the world and by sin death' (Romans 5: 12).
5. As Mary was free from original sin, there was no need for her to suffer corruption.
6. Christ would certainly not allow His mother to suffer corruption unnecessarily.
7. Therefore, although she may have died (in order to be more like her Son), her body did not suffer corruption.
8. It is therefore believed that she was assumed body and soul into heaven. This doctrine was believed for a long time but was only formally defined in 1950.

It is almost impossible to be fair in a brief summary of this kind, and I have deliberately arranged the successive stages in a manner which emphasizes my point; but I do not think I have unfairly represented any single one of them. To my mind, accustomed as I am to the scientific outlook, any step-by-step reasoning is notoriously liable to error and, unless successive steps are subjected to independent checks, the possible errors are multiplied with each step, so that the final conclusion is likely to be worthless. As I understand it, even the first step in this particular reasoning is a complete non-sequitur, the idea that Mary was necessarily without sin, 'original' or otherwise, being a philosophical artifact without any foundation in the Bible or anywhere else.

I suppose people are at liberty to hold any philosophical or theological ideas they like, however fanciful and unnecessary they may appear to others, but I do protest that such ideas should not be called 'Christian' unless they have some foundation in, or are fundamentally in keeping with Christ's teaching—the 'rock' upon which we ought to build. It is my opinion that the Virgin Mary cult is not so based. Indeed, I believe that the originators of this cult, whoever and whenever they may have been, developed it only by ignoring the teaching of Christ and adapting ideas from pagan religions, for with a profound knowledge of human nature, they deemed that their religion would make better progress if they had a woman in a prominent place in their theology. The Virgin Mary cult is how they got her there.

The purpose of this book is to plead for the principle that the teaching and example of Jesus constitute the primary authority for Christian faith and practice. For some time now there has been a most encouraging movement for reform within the Church of Rome, and it is to be hoped that those who inspire and direct it will hold to this principle as they seek to bring the Church's thinking up to date and find new ways of expressing the faith.

8 The Teaching of Jesus in the Synoptic Gospels

As has already been emphasized, there are in the four Gospels two different and irreconcilable versions of Christ's teaching. It is not possible to make a satisfactory synthesis of the two and the attempt to do so, as if they could be reconciled with one another, has done and still does much harm by encouraging intellectual dishonesty and pretence. We have to choose between the two versions, and the obvious and commonly accepted choice is in favour of the synoptic Gospels as representing the nearest we have to a literal, historical record, while the fourth Gospel is to be regarded as partly a supplement to the others and partly an interpretation of events in the light of the author's own thinking. The late Archbishop Temple likened the contrast to the difference between a photograph and a great painting; a painting may reveal truths in a way which a photograph cannot, but they are truths which spring from the artist's own interpretation of what he sees.

The reasons for this choice, from a layman's point of view, are that the synoptic Gospels were written earlier, that they represent the more or less consistent records of three compilers making use of several sources, and that the words of Jesus, in the main, have the appearance of remembered 'sayings' rather than discourses integrated with the compiler's own reasoning. The fourth Gospel, on the other hand, is generally agreed to have been written at least sixty years after the events, and reports the words of Jesus in such a way that they consistently and coherently support the 'axe' which the author quite frankly has to grind. For me there is the added, personal and not very scientific reason that the pronouncements and arguments which the author puts into the mouth of Jesus simply do not fit the kind of humility which I regard as typical of Jesus.

This relatively simple choice of the synoptics as against the fourth Gospel is necessary for the present purpose. I am fully aware that it is not possible to separate out the authentic words of Jesus from the rest of the record; and that some of the synoptic teachings quoted in this chapter are subject to doubt, while on the other hand much of the language of John may be authentic. But because it is impossible to make a satisfactory synthesis, some choice must be made, and for the present purpose it must be a simple one.

This conclusion does not seem to me to be invalidated by the modern view that the synoptic Gospels were probably compiled from collections of separate sayings or incidents which had been used in the Church for teaching purposes. The compilers must surely have used the most reliable versions available and included what they believed to be the most important events and teachings, arranged in the nearest they could get to chronological order (see Acts 1: 1).

This chapter, therefore, is an attempt to summarize the teaching of Jesus as it is found in the synoptic Gospels. We shall approach it in three stages: first some brief notes on the background in time and place; second, a short outline of the course of events according to these Gospels, with some indication of how the teaching of Jesus fitted into the pattern of events; and third, the teaching itself, in the actual words of the Gospels. It should be emphasized that in the synoptic accounts—whether we regard them as chronologically accurate or not—the teaching of Jesus is progressive, in the sense that the content and emphasis changes progressively with time; and is also conditioned by the progress of His ministry and the urgency of events.

BACKGROUND

Palestine was only a small part of the Roman Empire, about the size of Wales, but it was very troublesome to the occupying power, because of the religious obstinacy of the Jews, and consequently there were many changes in its administration. Jesus was born at the end of the reign of Herod the Great, who ruled a relatively large area and after whose death the kingdom was divided into four parts. At the time of the ministry of Jesus one part, the province of Judea, was governed directly by the Roman Procurator, while Galilee was part of the 'tetrarchy' of Herod Antipas. Samaria, the northern part of Judea, was inhabited by non-Jews, descendants of the foreigners who had been planted there by previous conquerors when the old northern kingdom of Israel was wiped out.

The past history of the Jews had been a chequered one, most of it spent under the suzerainty of one or other of the two great powers to East and West. The Jews lived in perpetual hope that one day God would send Messiah to save his people, but there were different degrees of expectation and different interpretations of what Messiah would be like.

The High Priests belonged to a wealthy Sadducean family and it suited them to keep on good terms with the Romans. At the other end of the scale were the Zealots—revolutionaries who were collecting weapons and making active preparations for revolt, and no doubt theirs was a popular point of view. There were others, however, who had a very different interpretation of Messiah—people like Mary and Joseph, Simeon and Anna, who were 'waiting for the consolation of Israel'. There were also more extreme ascetic sects, such as the Nazarites, who set themselves apart in separate communities, and it may well be that John the Baptist belonged to one of these.

Religion dominated the life of the country: taught in the home, practised in the synagogues, preached by the roadside, coming to dramatic focus in the great festivals centring in the Temple at Jerusalem, when Jews from all over the

Empire came together to fulfil their duties under the Law. It was to this turbulent little country, soaked in religious tradition, held down by the Romans but simmering with revolt, with wide extremes of simple peasant and sophisticated priest, ascetic prophet and learned scribe—all jostling for attention in so small a compass—that Jesus preached his gospel of the kingdom of God.

COURSE OF EVENTS

My aim is to outline what is found in the synoptic Gospels, without questioning the validity of any of the details, or considering the possibility that some of the incidents may have been exaggerated, or mythical, or later insertions, because these are matters on which I am not competent to judge.

According to Matthew and Luke, Jesus was born in Bethlehem in Judea and brought up in a carpenter's home at Nazareth in Galilee. At the age of about thirty He was baptized by John the Baptist and received a call from God. After this He spent a period of inner struggle in the wilderness and returned in the power of the Spirit ready to begin His ministry. He began teaching in the synagogues and outside, healing the sick in body and mind and preaching the gospel of the kingdom of God; collecting a number of disciples and choosing twelve of them to be His special companions. His whole campaign lasted for not more than three years and can conveniently be divided into four phases:

1. Healing and preaching, mainly in the towns and villages round the lake of Galilee, with rising popularity and increasing crowds, culminating in the test question to the apostles and the crowning experience of the transfiguration.

2. A journey by roundabout routes to Jerusalem, used for more sophisticated teaching and training of the apostles, with few healing miracles and a strong sense of urgency and impending crisis, culminating in the 'march on Jerusalem'.

3. A few days' intensive activity in the city, which in modern parlance might be called a one-man Direct Action Campaign, characterized by symbolic acts, test questions and arguments in the Temple precincts, and culminating in the arrest, trial and crucifixion.
4. The presence of the risen Jesus, in evidence of which only a few brief incidents are reported in the synoptic Gospels.

The overall time scale is uncertain and the order of events is slightly different in the three Gospels. Much of the teaching recorded is linked with particular incidents or questions, but the general tenor of it progressed with the changing events of His ministry, and was to some extent conditioned by Jesus' own state of mind. All this should be borne in mind in any attempt to interpret His teaching and apply it to our present age.

The selected passages which follow, expressed in the words of the New English Bible, represent an attempt to cover all important aspects of Christ's teaching in the synoptic Gospels. They are taken from all three Gospels and arranged mainly in the chronological order given by Luke, except that certain passages have been re-arranged in deference to the other two Gospels and that the Sermon on the Mount is given in Matthew's form.

(*A*) *Proclaiming the kingdom*

Luke 4: 17-21. He opened the scroll and found the passage which says:

'The spirit of the Lord is upon me because he has anointed me;
He has sent me to announce good news to the poor,
To proclaim release for prisoners and recovery of sight for the blind;
To let the broken victims go free,
To proclaim the year of the Lord's favour.'

He rolled up the scroll, gave it back to the attendant, and sat down; and all eyes in the synagogue were fixed on him.

He began to speak: 'Today', he said, 'in your very hearing this text has come true.'

Mark 1: 14-15. After John had been arrested, Jesus came into Galilee proclaiming the Gospel of God: 'The time has come; the kingdom of God is upon you; repent, and believe the Gospel.'

Luke 4: 40-43. At sunset all who had friends suffering from one disease or another brought them to him; and he laid his hands on them one by one and cured them. Devils also came out of many of them, shouting, 'You are the Son of God.' But he rebuked them and forbade them to speak, because they knew that he was the Messiah.

When day broke he went out and made his way to a lonely spot. But the people went in search of him, and when they came to where he was they pressed him not to leave them. But he said, 'I must give the good news of the kingdom of God to the other towns also, for that is what I was sent to do.'

(*B*) *Conflict with Tradition*—new wine versus old wine-skins.

Mark 2: 5-7. When Jesus saw their faith, he said to the paralysed man, 'My son, your sins are forgiven.'

Now there were some lawyers sitting there and they thought to themselves, 'Why does this fellow talk like this? This is blasphemy! Who but God alone can forgive sins?'

15-25. When Jesus was at table in his house, many bad characters—tax-gatherers and others—were seated with him and his disciples; for there were many who followed him. Some doctors of the law who were Pharisees noticed him eating in this bad company, and said to his disciples, 'He eats with tax-gatherers and sinners!' Jesus overheard and said to them, 'It is not the healthy that need a doctor, but the sick; I did not come to invite virtuous people, but sinners.'

Once, when John's disciples and the Pharisees were keeping a fast, some people came to him and said, 'Why is it that John's disciples and the disciples of the Pharisees are fasting, but yours are not?' Jesus said to them, 'Can you expect the bridegroom's friends to fast while the bridegroom is with them? As long as they have the bridegroom with them, there can be no fasting. But the time will come when the bridegroom will be taken away from them, and on that day they will fast.

'No one sews a patch of unshrunk cloth on to an old coat; if he does, the patch tears away from it, the new from the old, and leaves a bigger hole. No one puts new wine into old wine-skins; if he does, the wine will burst the skins, and then wine and skins are both lost. Fresh skins for new wine!'

One Sabbath he was going through the cornfields; and his disciples, as they went, began to pluck ears of corn. The Pharisees said to him, 'Look, why are they doing what is forbidden on the Sabbath?' . . .

27-28. He also said to them, 'The Sabbath was made for the sake of man and not man for the Sabbath: therefore the Son of Man is sovereign even over the Sabbath.'

(*C*) *The Sermon on the Mount*—outlining the values and standards of the kingdom.

(Only Matthew records all the teaching contained in the Sermon, which is given as a continuous discourse. The first part below is paralleled in Luke and other parts are scattered about Luke and Mark. The Sermon seems to have been addressed to the disciples, with the crowd 'listening in'.)

(1) *A New Scale of Values*

Matthew 5: 1-10. When he saw the crowds he went up the hill. There he took his seat, and when his disciples had gathered round him he began to address them. And this is the teaching he gave:

'How blest are those who know that they are poor;
the kingdom of Heaven is theirs.

How blest are the sorrowful;
they shall find consolation.

How blest are those of a gentle spirit;
they shall have the earth for their possession.

'How blest are those who hunger and thirst to see right prevail;
they shall be satisfied.

How blest are those who show mercy;
mercy shall be shown to them.

'How blest are those whose hearts are pure;
they shall see God.

How blest are the peacemakers;
God shall call them his sons.

How blest are those who have suffered persecution for the cause of right;
the kingdom of Heaven is theirs.'

13-16. 'You are salt to the world. And if salt becomes tasteless, how is its saltness to be restored? It is now good for nothing but to be thrown away and trodden underfoot.

'You are light for all the world. A town that stands on a hill cannot be hidden. When a lamp is lit, it is not put under the meal-tub, but on the lamp-stand, where it gives light to everyone in the house. And you, like the lamp, must shed light among your fellows, so that, when they see the good you do, they may give praise to your Father in Heaven.'

(2) *New Standards of Morality*—which 'complete' the law by going beyond the old legal requirements.

Matthew 5: 17-22. 'Do not suppose that I have come to abolish the Law and the prophets; I did not come to abolish, but to complete. I tell you this: so long as heaven and earth endure, not a letter, not a stroke, will disappear from the Law until all that must happen has happened. If any man therefore sets aside even the least of the Law's demands, and teaches others to do the same, he will have the lowest place in the kingdom of Heaven, whereas anyone who keeps the Law and teaches others so will stand high in the kingdom of Heaven. I tell you, unless you show yourselves far better men than the Pharisees and doctors of the law, you can never enter the kingdom of Heaven.

'You have learned that our forefathers were told, "Do not commit murder; anyone who commits murder must be brought to judgement." But what I tell you is this: Anyone who nurses anger against his brother must be brought to judgement. If he abuses his brother he must answer for it to the court; if he sneers at him he will have to answer for it in the fires of hell.'

27-28. 'You have learned that they were told, "Do not commit adultery." But what I tell you is this: If a man looks on a woman with a lustful eye, he has already committed adultery with her in his heart.'

31-37. 'They were told, "A man who divorces his wife must give her a note of dismissal." But what I tell you is this: If a man divorces his wife for any cause other than unchastity he involves her in adultery; and anyone who marries a woman so divorced commits adultery.

'Again, you have learned that they were told, "Do not break your oath", and, "Oaths sworn to the Lord must be kept." But what I tell you is this: You are not to swear at all—not by heaven, for it is God's throne, nor by earth, for it is his footstool, nor by Jerusalem, for it is the city of the great King, nor by your own head, because you cannot turn one hair of it white or black. Plain "Yes" or "No" is all you need to say; anything beyond that comes from the devil.'

(3) *A New Attitude to Personal Relationships and Material Possessions*, (in which the true 'blessedness' of the Beatitudes is found, and from which the new standards of morality derive their meaningfulness).

Matthew 5: 38-39. 'You have learned that they were told, "An eye for an eye, and a tooth for a tooth." But what I tell you is this: Do not set yourself against the man who wrongs you. If someone slaps you on the right cheek, turn and offer him your left.'

43-45, 48. 'You have learned that they were told, "Love your neighbour, hate your enemy." But what I tell you is this: Love your enemies and pray for your persecutors; only so can you be children of your heavenly Father, who makes his sun rise on good and bad alike, and sends the rain on the honest and the dishonest. . . . You must therefore be all goodness, just as your heavenly Father is all good.'

Matthew 6: 1-6. 'Be careful not to make a show of religion before men; if you do, no reward awaits you in your Father's house in heaven.

'Thus, when you do some act of charity, do not announce it with a flourish of trumpets, as the hypocrites do in synagogue and in the streets to win admiration from men. I tell you this: they have their reward already. No; when you do some act of charity, do not let your left hand know what your right hand is doing; your good deed must be secret, and your Father who sees what is done in secret will reward you.

'Again, when you pray, do not be like the hypocrites;

they love to say their prayers standing up in synagogue and at the street corners, for everyone to see them. I tell you this: they have their reward already. But when you pray, go into a room by yourself, shut the door, and pray to your Father who is there in the secret place; and your Father who sees what is secret will reward you.'

16-18. 'So too when you fast, do not look gloomy like the hypocrites: they make their faces unsightly so that other people may see that they are fasting. I tell you this: they have their reward already. But when you fast, anoint your head and wash your face, so that men may not see that you are fasting, but only your Father who is in the secret place; and your Father who sees what is secret will give you your reward.'

19-21. 'Do not store up for yourselves treasure on earth, where it grows rusty and moth-eaten, and thieves break in to steal it. Store up treasure in heaven, where there is no moth and no rust to spoil it, no thieves to break in and steal. For where your wealth is, there will your heart be also.'

24. 'No servant can be slave to two masters; for either he will hate the first and love the second, or he will be devoted to the first and think nothing of the second. You cannot serve God and Money.

25-30. 'Therefore I bid you put away anxious thoughts about food and drink to keep you alive, and clothes to cover your body. Surely life is more than food, the body more than clothes. Look at the birds of the air; they do not sow and reap and store in barns, yet your heavenly Father feeds them. You are worth more than the birds! Is there a man of you who by anxious thought can add a foot to his height? And why be anxious about clothes? Consider how the lilies grow in the fields; they do not work, they do not spin; and yet I tell you, even Solomon in all his splendour was not attired like one of these. But if that is how God clothes the grass in the fields, which is there today, and tomorrow is thrown on the stove, will he not all the more clothe you? How little faith you have!'

33-34. 'Set your mind on God's kingdom and his justice before everything else, and all the rest will come to you as well. So do not be anxious about tomorrow; tomorrow will look after itself. Each day has troubles enough of its own.

Matthew 7: 1-5. 'Pass no judgement, and you will not be judged. For as you judge others, so you will yourselves be judged, and whatever measure you deal out to others will be dealt back to you. Why do you look at the speck of sawdust in your brother's eye, with never a thought for the great plank in your own? Or how can you say to your brother, "Let me take the speck out of your eye", when all the time there is that plank in your own? You hypocrite! First take the plank out of your own eye, and then you will see clearly to take the speck out of your brother's.'

(4) *Summing up*

Matthew 7: 12-14. 'Always treat others as you would like them to treat you: that is the Law and the prophets.

'Enter by the narrow gate. The gate is wide that leads to perdition, there is plenty of room on the road, and many go that way; but the gate that leads to life is small and the road is narrow, and those who find it are few.'

21. 'Not everyone who calls me "Lord, Lord" will enter the kingdom of Heaven, but only those who do the will of my heavenly Father.'

24. 'What then of the man who hears these words of mine and acts upon them? He is like the man who had the sense to build his house on rock.'

(D) Faith and Healing

(A few incidents characteristic of the healing ministry of Jesus in this phase of his campaign, illustrating how he linked healing, and on one occasion, forgiveness, with faith.)

Luke 7: 2-10. A centurion there had a servant whom he valued highly; this servant was ill and near to death. Hearing about Jesus, he sent some Jewish elders with the request that he would come and save his servant's life. They approached Jesus and pressed their petition earnestly: 'He deserves this favour from you,' they said, 'for he is a friend of our nation and it is he who built us our synagogue.' Jesus went with them; but when he was not far from the house, the centurion sent friends with this message: 'Do not trouble further, sir; it is not for me to have you under my roof, and that is why I did not presume to approach you in person. But say the word and my servant will be cured. I know, for in my position I am myself under orders, with soldiers under me. I say to one, "Go", and he goes; to another, "Come here", and he comes; and to my servant, "Do this", and he does it.' When Jesus heard this, he admired the man, and, turning to the crowd that was following him, he said, 'I tell you, nowhere, even in Israel, have I found faith like this.' And the messengers returned to the house and found the servant in good health.

37, 44-50. A woman who was living an immoral life in the town had learned that Jesus was dining in the Pharisee's house and had brought oil of myrrh in a small flask. She took her place behind him, by his feet, weeping. . . .

Then turning to the woman, he said to Simon, 'You see this woman? I came to your house: you provided no water for my feet; but this woman has made my feet wet with her tears and wiped them with her hair. You gave me no kiss; but she has been kissing my feet ever since I came in. You did not anoint my head with oil; but she has anointed my feet with myrrh. And so, I tell you, her great love proves that her many sins have been forgiven; where little has been forgiven, little love is shown.' Then he said to her, 'Your sins are forgiven.' The other guests began to ask themselves, 'Who is this, that he can forgive sins?' But he said to the woman, 'Your faith has saved you; go in peace.'

Luke 8: 40-51. When Jesus returned, the people welcomed him, for they were all expecting him. Then a man appeared—Jairus was his name and he was president of the synagogue. Throwing himself down at Jesus's feet he begged him to come to his house, because he had an only daughter, about twelve years old, who was dying. And while Jesus was on his way he could hardly breathe for the crowds.

Among them was a woman who had suffered from haemorrhages for twelve years; and nobody had been able to cure her. She came up from behind and touched the edge of his cloak, and at once her haemorrhage stopped. Jesus said, 'Who was it that touched me?' All disclaimed it, and Peter and his companions said, 'Master, the crowds are hemming you in and pressing upon you!' But Jesus said, 'Someone did touch me, for I felt that power had gone out from me.' Then the woman, seeing that she was detected, came trembling and fell at his feet. Before all the people she explained why she had touched him and how she had been instantly cured. He said to her, 'My daughter, your faith has cured you. Go in peace.'

While he was still speaking, a man from the president's house came with the message, 'Your daughter is dead; trouble the Rabbi no further.' But Jesus heard and interposed. 'Do not be afraid,' he said; 'only show faith and she will be well again.'

Matthew 17: 20. 'I tell you this: if you have faith no bigger even than a mustard-seed, you will say to this mountain, "Move from here to there!", and it will move; nothing will prove impossible for you.'

(*E*) *Sowing the Seed*

(The healing mission went on and Jesus's fame continued to spread, but this was no real answer to the problem of the 'propagation' of the kingdom of God. Jesus gave an inkling of the answer in some of the parables of the kingdom and in his first experiment in the delegation of power.)

Luke 8: 1. After this he went journeying from town to town and village to village, proclaiming the good news of the kingdom of God.

Matthew 13: 4-9. He said: 'A sower went out to sow. And as he sowed, some seed fell along the footpath; and the birds came and ate it up. Some seed fell on rocky ground, where it had little soil; it sprouted quickly because it had no depth of earth, but when the sun rose the young corn was scorched, and as it had no root it withered away. Some seed fell among thistles; and the thistles shot up, and choked the corn. And some of the seed fell into good soil, where it bore fruit, yielding a hundredfold or, it might be, sixtyfold or thirtyfold. If you have ears, then hear.'

24-30. Here is another parable that he put before them: 'The kingdom of Heaven is like this. A man sowed his field with good seed; but while everyone was asleep his enemy came, sowed darnel among the wheat, and made off. When the corn sprouted and began to fill out, the darnel could be seen among it. The farmer's men went to their master and said, "Sir, was it not good seed that you sowed in your field? Then when has the darnel come from?" "This is an enemy's doing", he replied. "Well then," they said, "Shall we go and gather the darnel?" "No", he answered; "in gathering it you might pull up the wheat at the same time. Let them both grow together till harvest; and at harvest-time I will tell the reapers, 'Gather the darnel first, and tie it in bundles for burning; then collect the wheat into my barn.'

31-33. And this is another parable he put before them: 'The kingdom of Heaven is like mustard-seed, which a man took and sowed in his field. As a seed, mustard is smaller than any other; but when it is grown it is bigger than any garden plant; it becomes a tree, big enough for the birds to come and roost among its branches.'

He told them also this parable: 'The kingdom of Heaven is like yeast, which a woman took and mixed with half a hundredweight of flour till it was all leavened.'

44-50. 'The kingdom of Heaven is like treasure lying buried in a field. The man who found it, buried it again; and for sheer joy went and sold everything he had, and bought that field.

'Here is another picture of the kingdom of Heaven. A merchant looking out for fine pearls found one of very special value; so he went and sold everything he had, and bought it.

'Again the kingdom of Heaven is like a net let down into the sea, where fish of every kind were caught in it. When it was full, it was dragged ashore. Then the men sat down and collected the good fish into pails and threw the worthless away. That is how it will be at the end of time. The angels will go forth, and they will separate the wicked from the good, and throw them into the blazing furnace, the place of wailing and grinding of teeth.'

(In Luke some of these parables appear at a later stage, but Mark gives them before the sending out of the twelve.)

Mark 6: 7-13. On one of his teaching journeys round the villages he summoned the Twelve and sent them out in pairs on a mission. He gave them authority over unclean spirits, and instructed them to take nothing for the journey beyond a stick: no bread, no pack, no money in their belts. They might wear sandals, but not a second coat. 'When you are admitted to a house', he added, 'stay there until you leave those parts. At any place where they will not receive you or listen to you, shake the dust off your feet as you leave, as a warning to them.' So they set out and called publicly for repentance. They drove out many devils, and many sick people they anointed with oil and cured.

(F) The Turning Point

(After not more than two and a half years of campaigning, Jesus put the test question to his disciples. On receiving a satisfactory answer, He must have decided to 'go to Jerusalem'—i.e., to bring the campaign to a climax coinciding with the Passover.)

Mark 8: 27-36. Jesus and his disciples set out for the villages of Caesarea Philippi. On the way he asked his disciples, 'Who do men say I am?' They answered, 'Some say John the Baptist, others Elijah, others one of the prophets.' 'And you,' he asked, 'who do you say I am?' Peter replied: 'You are the Messiah.' Then he gave them strict orders not to tell anyone about him; and he began to teach them that the Son of Man had to undergo great sufferings, and to be rejected by the elders, chief priests, and doctors of the law; to be put to death, and to rise again three days afterwards. He spoke about it plainly. At this Peter took him by the arm and began to rebuke him. But Jesus turned round, and, looking at his disciples, rebuked Peter. 'Away with you, Satan,' he said; 'you think as men think, not as God thinks.'

Then he called the people to him, as well as his disciples, and said to them, 'Anyone who wishes to be a follower of mine must leave self behind; he must take up his cross, and come with me. Whoever cares for his own safety is lost; but if a man will let himself be lost for my sake and for the Gospel, that man is safe. What does a man gain by winning the whole world at the cost of his true self?'

Mark 9: 1. He also said, 'I tell you this: there are some of those standing here who will not taste death before they have seen the kingdom of God already come in power.'

(Six days later came the transfiguration, followed by renewed warning to the disciples of what was to come.)

Mark 9: 30-32. They now left that district and made a journey through Galilee. Jesus wished it to be kept secret; for he was teaching his disciples, and telling them, 'The Son of Man is now to be given up into the power of men, and they will kill him, and three days after being killed he will rise again.' But they did not understand what he said, and were afraid to ask.

42-48. 'As for the man who leads astray one of these little ones who have faith, it would be better for him to be thrown into the sea with a millstone round his neck. If your hand is your undoing, cut it off; it is better for you to enter into life maimed than to keep both hands and go to hell and the unquenchable fire. And if it is your foot that leads you astray, cut it off; it is better for you to enter into life a cripple than to keep both your feet and be thrown into hell. And if it is your eye, tear it out; it is better to enter into the kingdom of God with one eye than to keep both eyes and be thrown into hell, where the devouring worm never dies and the fire is not quenched.

(G) Pilgrimage to Jerusalem

(There is a great sense of urgency here. Jesus sent the seventy on ahead to spread the message as widely as possible while there was yet time. This was a second experiment in the delegation of power and Jesus, like the disciples, was clearly delighted at the success of it.)

Luke 10: 1-5. After this the Lord appointed a further seventy-two and sent them on ahead in pairs to every town and place he was going to visit himself. He said to them: 'The crop is heavy, but labourers are scarce; you must therefore beg the owner to send labourers to harvest his crop. Be on your way. And look, I am sending you like lambs among wolves. Carry no purse or pack, and travel barefoot. Exchange no greetings on the road.

10-11. 'When you enter a town and they do not make you welcome, go out into its streets and say, "The very dust of your town that clings to our feet we wipe off to your shame. Only take note of this: the kingdom of God has come close." '

17-19. The seventy-two came back jubilant. 'In your name, Lord,' they said, 'even the devils submit to us.' He replied, 'I watched how Satan fell, like lightning, out of the sky. And now you see that I have given you the power to tread underfoot snakes and scorpions and all the forces of the enemy, and nothing will ever harm you.'

23-24. Turning to his disciples in private he said, 'Happy the eyes that see what you are seeing! I tell you, many prophets and kings wished to see what you now see, yet never saw it; to hear what you hear, yet never heard it.'

Luke 11: 14-15, 19-20. He was driving out a devil which was dumb; and when the devil had come out, the dumb man began to speak. The people were astonished, but some of them said, 'It is by Beelzebub prince of devils that he drives the devils out.' . . .

(Jesus said) 'If it is by Beelzebub that I cast out devils, by whom do your own people drive them out? If this is your argument, they themselves will refute you. But if it is by the finger of God that I drive out the devils, then be sure the kingdom of God has already come upon you.'

(There follow miscellaneous teachings, some in response to particular questions or incidents, some probably a continuation of the disciples' training.)

The Great Commandments

Luke 10: 25-30, 36-37. On one occasion a lawyer came forward to put this test question to him: 'Master, what must I do to inherit eternal life?' Jesus said, 'What is written in the Law? What is your reading of it?' He replied, 'Love the Lord your God with all your heart, with all your soul, with all your strength, and with all your mind; and your neighbour as yourself.' 'That is the right answer,' said Jesus; 'do that, and you will live.'

But he wanted to vindicate himself, so he said to Jesus, 'And who is my neighbour?'

(Then follows the parable of the Good Samaritan.)

. . . 'Which of these three do you think was neighbour to the man who fell into the hands of the robbers?' He answered, 'The one who showed him kindness.' Jesus said, 'Go and do as he did.'

Prayer

Matthew 6: 9-15.

'This is how you should pray:
"Our Father in heaven,
Thy name be hallowed;
Thy kingdom come,
Thy will be done,
On earth as in heaven.
Give us today our daily bread.
Forgive us the wrong we have done,
As we have forgiven those who have wronged us.
And do not bring us to the test,
But save us from the evil one."

'For if you forgive others the wrong they have done, your heavenly Father will also forgive you; but if you do not forgive others, then the wrongs you have done will not be forgiven by your Father.'

Luke 11: 5-10. He added, 'Suppose one of you has a friend who comes to him in the middle of the night and says, "My friend, lend me three loaves, for a friend of mine on a journey has turned up at my house, and I have nothing to offer him"; and he replies from inside, "Do not bother me. The door is shut for the night; my children and I have gone to bed; and I cannot get up and give you what you want." I tell you that even if he will not provide for him out of friendship, the very shamelessness of the request will make him get up and give him all he needs. And so I say to you, ask, and you will receive; seek, and you will find; knock, and the door will be opened. For everyone who asks receives, he who seeks finds, and to him who knocks, the door will be opened.'

Condemnation of Pharisees and Lawyers

Luke 11: 37-46, 52. When he had finished speaking, a Pharisee invited him to dinner. He came in and sat down. The Pharisee noticed with surprise that he had not begun by washing before the meal. But the Lord said to him, 'You Pharisees! You clean the outside of cup and plate; but inside you there is nothing but greed and wickedness. You fools! Did not he who made the outside make the inside too? But let what is in the cup be given in charity, and all is clean.

'Alas for you Pharisees! You pay tithes of mint and rue and every garden-herb, but have no care for justice and the love of God. It is these you should have practised, without neglecting the others.

'Alas for you Pharisees! You love the seats of honour in synagogues, and salutations in the market-places.

'Alas, alas, you are like unmarked graves over which men may walk without knowing it.'

In reply to this one of the lawyers said, 'Master, when you say things like this you are insulting us too.' Jesus rejoined: 'Yes, you lawyers, it is no better with you! For you load men with intolerable burdens, and will not put a single finger to the load.'. . .

'Alas for you lawyers! You have taken away the key of knowledge. You did not go in yourselves, and those who were on their way in, you stopped.'

Warnings and encouragement

(At this stage in Luke's Gospel, warnings of the cost of discipleship and of the coming crisis are linked with the teaching on trust in God which we have already quoted in Matthew's version of the Sermon on the Mount.)

Luke 12: 1-2, 4-12. Meanwhile, when a crowd of many thousands had gathered, packed so close that they were treading on one another, he began to speak first to his disciples: 'Beware of the leaven of the Pharisees; I mean their hypocrisy. There is nothing covered up that will not be uncovered, nothing hidden that will not be made known. . . .

'To you who are my friends I say: Do not fear those who kill the body and after that have nothing more they can do. I will warn you whom to fear: fear him who, after he has killed, has authority to cast into hell. Believe me, he is the one to fear.

'Are not sparrows five for twopence? And yet not one of them is overlooked by God. More than that, even the hairs of your head have all been counted. Have no fear; you are worth more than any number of sparrows.

'I tell you this: everyone who acknowledges me before men, the Son of Man will acknowledge before the angels of God; but he who disowns me before men will be disowned before the angels of God.

'Anyone who speaks a word against the Son of Man will receive forgiveness; but for him who slanders the Holy Spirit there will be no forgiveness.

'When you are brought before synagogues and state authorities, do not begin worrying about how you will conduct your defence or what you will say. For when the time comes the Holy Spirit will instruct you what to say.'

31-40. '. . . No, set your mind upon his kingdom, and all the rest will come to you as well.

'Have no fear, little flock; for your Father has chosen to give you the Kingdom. Sell your possessions and give in charity. Provide for yourselves purses that do not wear out, and never-failing wealth in heaven, where no thief can get near it, no moth destroy it. For where your wealth is, there will your heart be also.

'Be ready for action, with belts fastened and lamps alight. Be like men who wait for their master's return from a wedding-party, ready to let him in the moment he arrives and knocks. Happy are those servants whom the master finds on the alert when he comes. I tell you this: he will buckle his belt, seat them at table, and come and wait on them. Even if it is the middle of the night or before dawn when he comes, happy they if he finds them alert. And remember, if the householder had known what time the burglar was coming he would not have let his house be broken into. Hold yourselves ready, then, because the Son of Man is coming at the time you least expect him.'

49-56. 'I have come to set fire to the earth, and how I wish it were already kindled! I have a baptism to undergo, and how hampered I am until the ordeal is over! Do you suppose I came to establish peace on the earth? No indeed, I have come to bring division. For from now on, five members of a family will be divided, three against two and two against three; father against son and son against father, mother against daughter and daughter against mother, mother against son's wife and son's wife against her mother-in-law.'

He also said to the people, 'When you see cloud banking up in the west, you say at once, "It is going to rain", and rain it does. And when the wind is from the south you say, "There will be a heat-wave", and there is. What hypocrites you are! You know how to interpret the appearance of earth and sky; how is it you cannot interpret this fateful hour?'

Luke 13: 22-24, 29-30. He continued his journey through towns and villages, teaching as he made his way towards Jerusalem. Someone asked him, 'Sir, are only a few to be saved?' His answer was: 'Struggle to get in through the narrow door; for I tell you that many will try to enter and not be able. . . .

'From east and west people will come, from north and south, for the feast in the kingdom of God. Yes, and some who are now last will be first, and some who are first will be last.'

Luke 14: 25-30, 33. Once when great crowds were accompanying him, he turned to them and said: 'If anyone comes to me and does not hate his father and mother, wife and children, brothers and sisters, even his own life, he cannot be a disciple of mine. No one who does not carry his cross and come with me can be a disciple of mine. Would any of you think of building a tower without first sitting down and calculating the cost, to see whether he could afford to finish it? Otherwise, if he has laid its foundation and then is not able to complete it, all the onlookers will laugh at him. "There is a man", they will say, "who started to build and could not finish.". . .

'So also none of you can be a disciple of mine without taking leave of all his possessions.'

God's care for the lost

Luke 15: 1-13, 31-32. Another time, the tax-gatherers and other bad characters were all crowding in to listen to him; and the Pharisees and the doctors of the law began grumbling among themselves: 'This fellow', they said, 'welcomes sinners and eats with them.' He answered them with this parable: 'If one of you has a hundred sheep and loses one of them, does he not leave the ninety-nine in the open pasture and go after the missing one until he has found it? How delighted he is then! He lifts it on to his shoulders, and home he goes to call his friends and neighbours together. "Rejoice with me!" he cries. "I have found my lost sheep." In the same way, I tell you, there will be greater joy in heaven over one sinner who repents than over ninety-nine righteous people who do not need to repent.

'Or again, if a woman has ten silver pieces and loses one of them, does she not light the lamp, sweep out the house, and look in every corner till she has found it? And when she has, she calls her friends and neighbours together, and says, "Rejoice with me! I have found the piece that I lost." In the same way, I tell you, there is joy among the angels of God over one sinner who repents.'

Again he said: 'There was once a man who had two sons; and the younger said to his father, "Father, give me my share of the property." So he divided his estate between them. . . .'

(Here follows the story of the Prodigal Son)

' "My boy," said the father, "you are always with me, and everything I have is yours. How could we help celebrating this happy day? Your brother here was dead and has come back to life, was lost and is found." '

Luke 19: 9-10. (The conversion of Zacchaeus)

Jesus said to him, 'Salvation has come to this house today!—for this man too is a son of Abraham, and the Son of Man has come to seek and save what is lost.'

Qualifications for the kingdom

Luke 18: 10-14. 'Two men went up to the temple to pray, one a Pharisee and the other a tax-gatherer. The Pharisee stood up and prayed thus: "I thank thee, O God, that I am not like the rest of men, greedy, dishonest, adulterous; or, for that matter, like this tax-gatherer. I fast twice a week; I pay tithes on all that I get." But the other kept his distance and would not even raise his eyes to heaven, but beat upon his breast, saying, "O God, have mercy on me, sinner that I am." It was this man, I tell you, and not the other, who went home acquitted of his sins. For everyone who exalts himself will be humbled; and whoever humbles himself will be exalted.'

15-17. They even brought babies for him to touch; but when the disciples saw them they scolded them for it. But Jesus called for the children and said, 'Let the little ones come to me; do not try to stop them; for the kingdom of God belongs to such as these. I tell you that whoever does not accept the kingdom of God like a child will never enter it.'

18-25. A man of the ruling class put this question to him: 'Good Master, what must I do to win eternal life?' Jesus said to him, 'Why do you call me good? No one is good except God alone. You know the commandments: "Do not commit adultery; do not murder; do not steal; do not give false evidence; honour your father and mother." ' The man answered, 'I have kept all these since I was a boy.' On hearing this Jesus said, 'There is still one thing lacking; sell everything you have and distribute to the poor, and you will have riches in heaven; and come, follow me.' At these words his heart sank; for he was a very rich man.

When Jesus saw it he said, 'How hard it is for the wealthy to enter the kingdom of God! It is easier for a camel to go through the eye of a needle than for a rich man to enter the kingdom of God.'

Matthew 20: 20-21, 24-28. The mother of Zebedee's sons then came before him, with her sons. She bowed low and begged a favour. 'What is it you wish?', asked Jesus. 'I want you', she said, 'to give orders that in your kingdom my two sons here may sit next to you, one at your right and the other your left.' . . .

When the other ten heard this, they were indignant with the two brothers. So Jesus called them to him and said, 'You know that in the world, rulers lord it over their subjects, and their great men make them feel the weight of authority; but it shall not be so with you. Among you, whoever wants to be great must be your servant, and whoever would be first must be the willing slave of all—like the Son of Man; he did not come to be served, but to serve, and to surrender his life as a ransom for many.'

Matthew 25: 31-36, 40.

(This parable is actually given later, in Jerusalem, but I have brought it forward because it fits in with the theme of the foregoing.)

'When the Son of Man comes in his glory and all the angels with him, he will sit in state on his throne, with all the nations gathered before him. He will separate men into two groups, as a shepherd separates the sheep from the goats, and he will place the sheep on his right hand and the goats on his left. Then the king will say to those on his right hand, "You have my Father's blessing; come, enter and possess the kingdom that has been ready for you since the world was made. For when I was hungry, you gave me food; when thirsty, you gave me drink; when I was a stranger you took me into your home, when naked you clothed me; when

I was ill you came to my help, when in prison you visited me . . .

' "I tell you this: anything you did for one of my brothers here, however humble, you did for me." '

(H) The Messiah: Challenge and warning to the city

(The symbolic ride into Jerusalem, in fulfilment of a prophecy—'Behold, your king cometh, meek and riding upon an ass'—was, according to the synoptic Gospels, Jesus' first public claim to be Messiah. It is interesting to note that when the apostles earlier recognized his Messiahship Jesus immediately warned them, privately, of troubles and sufferings to come, and repeated these warnings on the way to Jerusalem, while still refraining from any public prophecies of destruction. After the triumphal entry, in which he publicly claimed to be Messiah and was publicly recognized as such, he publicly and emphatically warned of the coming destruction of Jerusalem—which actually came to pass in A.D. 70; privately, to the disciples, he linked this in apocalyptic terms with the end of the age and the coming of the Son of Man, all of which he predicted in the near future.)

Luke 18: 31-34. He took the Twelve aside and said, 'We are going up to Jerusalem; and all that was written by the prophets will come true for the Son of Man. He will be handed over to the foreign power. He will be mocked, maltreated, and spat upon. They will flog him and kill him. And on the third day he will rise again.' But they understood nothing of this; they did not grasp what he was talking about; its meaning was concealed from them.

Luke 19: 35-38. . . . So they brought the colt to Jesus.

Then they threw their cloaks on the colt, for Jesus to mount, and they carpeted the road with them as he went on his way. And now, as he approached the descent from the Mount of Olives, the whole company of his disciples in their joy began to sing aloud the praises of God for all the things they had seen: 'Blessings on him who comes as king in the name of the Lord! Peace in heaven, glory in highest heaven!'

41-46. When he came in sight of the city, he wept over it and said, 'If only you had known, on this great day, the way that leads to peace! But no; it is hidden from your sight. For a time will come upon you, when your enemies will set up siege-works against you; they will encircle you and hem you in at every point; they will bring you to the ground, you and your children within your walls, and not leave you one stone standing on another, because you did not recognize God's moment when it came.'

Then he went into the temple and began driving out the traders, with these words: 'Scripture says, "My house shall be a house of prayer"; but you have made it a robbers' cave.'

Mark 13: 1-10. As he was leaving the temple, one of his disciples exclaimed, 'Look, Master, what huge stones! What fine buildings!' Jesus said to him, 'You see these great buildings? Not one stone will be left upon another; all will be thrown down.'

When he was sitting on the Mount of Olives facing the temple he was questioned privately by Peter, James, John, and Andrew. 'Tell us,' they said, 'when will this happen? What will be the sign when the fulfilment of all this is at hand?'

Jesus began: 'Take care that no one misleads you. Many will come claiming my name, and saying, "I am he"; and many will be misled by them.

'When you hear the noise of battle near at hand and the news of battles far away, do not be alarmed. Such things are bound to happen; but the end is still to come. For nation will make war upon nation, kingdom upon kingdom; there will be earthquakes in many places; there will be famines. With these things the birth pangs of the new age begin.

'As for you, be on your guard. You will be handed over to the courts. You will be flogged in synagogues. You will be summoned to appear before governors and kings on my account to testify in their presence. But before the end the Gospel must be proclaimed to all nations.'

14. 'But when you see "the abomination of desolation" usurping a place which is not his* (let the reader understand), then those who are in Judea must take to the hills.'

20. 'If the Lord had not cut short that time of troubles, no living thing could survive. However, for the sake of his own, whom he has chosen, he has cut short the time.'

24-31. 'But in those days, after that distress, the sun will be darkened, the moon will not give her light; the stars will come falling from the sky, the celestial powers will be shaken. Then they will see the Son of Man coming in the clouds with great power and glory, and he will send out the angels and gather his chosen from the four winds, from the farthest bounds of earth to the farthest bounds of heaven.

'Learn a lesson from the fig-tree. When its tender shoots appear and are breaking into leaf, you know that summer is near. In the same way, when you see all this happening, you may know that the end is near, at the very door. I tell you this: the present generation will live to see it all. Heaven and earth will pass away; my words will never pass away.

Mark 14: 22-25 (The last supper)

During supper he took bread, and having said the blessing he broke it and gave it to them, with the

* when a pagan standard is set up in the temple.

words: 'Take this; this is my body.' Then he took a cup, and having offered thanks to God he gave it to them; and they all drank from it. And he said, 'This is my blood of the covenant, shed for many. I tell you this: never again shall I drink from the fruit of the vine until that day when I drink it new in the kingdom of God.'

Luke 22: 67-70 (The examination by the Council)

'Tell us,' they said, 'are you the Messiah?' 'If I tell you,' he replied, 'you will not believe me; and if I ask questions, you will not answer. But from now on, the Son of Man will be seated at the right hand of Almighty God.' 'You are the Son of God, then?' they all said, and he replied, 'It is you who say I am.' They said, 'Need we call further witnesses? We have heard it ourselves from his own lips.'

Luke 23: 3 (The trial before Pilate)

Pilate asked him, 'Are you the king of the Jews?' He replied, 'The words are yours.'

(*I*) *The resurrection commission*

Luke 24: 25-27 (on the road to Emmaus)

'How dull you are!' he answered. 'How slow to believe all that the prophets said! Was the Messiah not bound to suffer thus before entering upon his glory?' Then he began with Moses and all the prophets, and explained to them the passages which referred to himself in every part of the scriptures.

Luke 24: 44-49. And he said to them, 'This is what I meant by saying, while I was still with you, that everything written about me in the Law of Moses and in the prophets and psalms was bound to be fulfilled.' Then he opened their minds to understand the scriptures. 'This', he said, 'is what is written: that the Messiah is to suffer death and to rise from the dead on the third day, and that in his name repentance bringing the forgiveness of sins is to be proclaimed to all nations. Begin from Jerusalem: it is you who are the witnesses to all this. And mark this: I am sending upon you my Father's promised gift; so stay here in this city until you are armed with the power from above.'

Matthew 28: 16-20. The eleven disciples made their way to Galilee, to the mountain where Jesus had told them to meet him. When they saw him, they fell prostrate before him, though some were doubtful. Jesus then came up and spoke to them. He said: 'Full authority in heaven and on earth has been committed to me. Go forth therefore and make all nations my disciples; baptize men everywhere in the name of the Father and the Son and the Holy Spirit, and teach them to observe all that I have commanded you. And be assured, I am with you always, to the end of time.'

(There is a discrepancy between the last two passages. According to Luke's version, Jesus gave the final commissioning in Jerusalem, from which he led the disciples out to Bethany, where he parted from them. In Matthew's account the commissioning took place on a mountain in Galilee.)

9 Some Exploratory Notes

BEFORE commenting on the teaching summarized in the last chapter, it is necessary to make two preliminary observations. Jesus did not write a book outlining His teaching and neither did the writers of the synoptic Gospels. What they did was to set down the important facts about Jesus, according to their own sources of information, and the teaching is part of this record. Although in the last chapter I have tried to extract it from the record in such a way that, as nearly as possible, it stands on its own, these extracts, as they stand, do not of course form an outline of the teaching of Jesus.

In the first place there was a logical development in His teaching which was suited to His own hearers and His own time, and is not necessarily appropriate for us in our time. He started with simple declarations and, on the whole, proceeded step by step to more sophisticated explanations, the progress being dependent on what His hearers could absorb. It is clear that at times Jesus held back parts of His message until He was quite sure that His hearers were ready to receive them, and proceeded from stage to stage on this basis; but He progressed at two different speeds simultaneously—one with His intimate band of disciples, the other with 'the crowd'.

Jesus was speaking to people who believed in God without question and who also believed that God would send Messiah to save His people, but their conception of Messiah was so different from His that although, according to the records, He felt Himself to be Messiah from the start of His ministry, He did not publicly declare it until the end. His early preaching seems to have been in very simple terms, with actions that spoke louder than words; the main impact on the ordinary people who saw and heard Him would be twofold:

1. The sense that something big was happening here and now, history coming to a climax: 'The time has come', and
2. The compelling evidence of healing miracles—good power at work against the evil powers with which they were so familiar.

These two combined to swell the crowds and produce His rising popularity. Crowds always like to be present when history is in the making—to be near to the great. Miracles are always popular and everything He did had news value. And the people whose lives were actually transformed by His healing would learn a deeper attachment to His message, whether they understood the message or not. When a few guessed at His Messiahship He told them to keep quiet about it, presumably on the ground that the idea was too dangerous until the time had come to show what it really meant.

For the greater part of His ministry even His intimate band of followers were not told this secret. Only after they had lived and campaigned with Him for a couple of years and had themselves gone out to preach and exercise the same power that He did, were they ready for the test question, 'Who do you say I am?', and Peter's reply, 'You are the Messiah'. Then after giving them strict orders to keep it secret, He slammed down the challenge of what Messiahship really meant: that the Son of Man had to undergo great sufferings, and to be rejected by the elders, chief priests and doctors of the law; to be put to death and to rise again. From then on Jesus was free to tell them, but not the crowd, of the sufferings to come, for Himself and for all who followed Him.

With the triumphal entry into Jerusalem Jesus was, in effect, asking the public the same test question. Many recognized the reference and responded by hailing Him as

Messiah. Immediately after this He threw down the same kind of challenge in public, prophesying sufferings to come and the destruction of the city.

It is clear therefore that some parts of the teaching belong specifically to particular stages in this progressive revelation, and it would be quite misleading to take slices of it out of the context and ignore the appropriate background. Here is an obvious example: 'If anyone comes to me and does not hate his father and mother, wife and children . . . he cannot be a disciple of mine. . . . So also, none of you can be a disciple of mine without taking leave of all his possessions.' These words were spoken within a few days of His death. As crowds flocked to hear and follow Him, He issued a clear warning that anyone who chose to become a disciple of His at that particular time was taking his life in his hands and must leave everything but discipleship behind. It would obviously be highly misleading to take the words out of this context and state as part of the teaching of Jesus that every Christian must sever his family relationships and give up all his possessions.

The second thing which needs to be said before attempting to interpret Christ's teaching is that His message was a 'crisis' message in the sense that, right up to the time of His death, He spoke and acted as if time had very nearly run out, and 'this world'—the ordinary world of people, nations and empires—was very near to its end.

He began with the phrase 'The time has come' and emphasized again and again that the kingdom of God was close at hand—whatever that meant. But it was clear that His own campaign in Palestine was—as He saw it—only the first step in God's decisive and final intervention in the affairs of men. After His death the Gospel of the kingdom would be preached throughout the world, calling men and women everywhere to repentance, and then, after great conflicts and sufferings, God would 'bring in' His kingdom in a very different and cataclysmic sense, with the Son of Man playing a central rôle. And all this would happen soon.

In the event, heaven and earth did not pass away, and it is meaningless to postpone this crisis to some indefinite distant future—but more of that later. For the present purpose the point is that Christ's teaching was set in a crisis context and was all of a piece with the statement that God would intervene catastrophically and decisively, then in that generation. When we come to apply His teaching to a later age, this fact must be taken into account.

Having made these two preliminary points I shall try in the remainder of this chapter to highlight what seem to me to be the important themes of His teaching, dealing very briefly with those which are obvious and well known and, at somewhat greater length, with some which seem to me to need further emphasis or explanation. I shall take the themes in the chronological order adopted in Chapter 8 because this shows a logical development in the teaching, at least in the first phase of His ministry; though to some extent the logical development may be the result of the Gospel-writers' arrangement rather than the actual order of Christ's teaching.

THE KINGDOM OF GOD

In the synoptic Gospels the central theme of Christ's teaching—or, to put it another way, the framework into which his teachings about God, man and eternal life were fitted—is the kingdom of God, or the kingdom of Heaven; the two titles seem to be used interchangeably, Matthew's Gospel favouring the latter. It is a confusing concept for modern minds, partly because we seem to have no single phrase expressing it which has much impact on everyday life.

The idea of the kingdom of God was well established in the Old Testament, where already it was thought of in two senses, present and future. In the present sense it meant God's rule over the nations, whether they acknowledged Him or not:

'For dominion belongs to the Lord, and he rules over the nations. (Psalm 22)

'The Lord has established his throne in the heavens, and his kingdom rules over all.' (Psalm 103)

Isaiah saw God using other nations as tools to punish His chosen people:

'He will raise a signal for a nation afar off, and whistle for it from the ends of the earth; and lo, swiftly, speedily it comes!'

God's kingdom was over the whole world and history was the record of his acts:

'Thine, O Lord, is the greatness, and the power, and the glory, and the victory, and the majesty; for all that is in the heavens and in the earth is thine; thine is the kingdom, O Lord, and thou art exalted as head above all.' (1 Chronicles 29)

But the kingdom of God had a future sense in the Old Testament, too, though it was not described in the same terms. The great prophets looked forward to the day when God would vindicate His power and restore His chosen people to their rightful place among the nations; and Messiah would be the instrument of that new kind of kingdom of God on earth:

'Of the increase of his government and of peace there will be no end, upon the throne of David, and over his kingdom, to establish it and to uphold it with justice and with righteousness from this time forth and for ever more . . .' (Isaiah 9)

'In that day the root of Jesse shall stand as an ensign to the peoples; him shall the nations seek, and his dwellings shall be glorious.' (Isaiah 11)

'Lo, your king comes to you; triumphant and victorious is he, humble and riding on an ass, on a colt the foal of an ass . . .

'And he shall command peace to the nations; his dominion shall be from sea to sea, and from the River to the ends of the earth.' (Zechariah 9)

Jesus adopted the Old Testament conception of the kingdom of God and put entirely new meanings into it.

He described and illustrated it in so many different ways that the picture is really rather confusing, but behind all the illustrations, though not always emerging clearly in the records, were the two quite distinct meanings:

1. God's sphere of influence here and now, and
2. A future 'eternal' kingdom, reserved for those accounted worthy of it.

Jesus began with the first meaning and transformed it. He brought the good news that God's rule, presence, power, sphere of influence—the same power and sovereignty which still ruled nations and made history—was here and now, something to be entered into and experienced by ordinary people, a treasure beyond price.

It is as though you tried to explain to some primitive man the marvels of electricity and decided to begin with a fact of electricity with which he would be familiar—lightning. The 'kingdom of lightning', you would explain, is not only something which rends the heavens and puts fear into the heart of man. It is also 'at hand'—around us, available for us, even in us. You would demonstrate electricity at work in everyday life—a torch, the switching on of a light, a television set; if you had access to the right equipment, you might even demonstrate the electric currents in his own brain—electricity at the very ground of our being. So the 'kingdom of lightning' enters into ordinary everyday life—not a hundred million volts of it, but whatever quantity may be appropriate to our needs.

So Jesus proclaimed and demonstrated that the rule of God was not only for the control of nations, from His throne in the heavens; it was 'at hand' in the sense of time—a focusing of history upon that very moment, but also 'at hand' in the sense of nearness, availability—something for everyone to enter into and enjoy.

His early ministry began with miracles of healing and 'casting out devils'—miracles which cannot be separated from His teaching because they were the first dramatic impact of that teaching. They demonstrated the here-and-nowness of God's power for good and Jesus emphasized this point again and again. At the outset when crowds from Capernaum pressed Him to stay and continue His ministry of healing, He excused Himself by saying: 'I must give the good news of the kingdom of God to the other towns also.' At this stage the healing ministry *was* the good news of the kingdom of God. Much later, when He sent out the seventy on a healing mission into new districts, to declare the gospel in the same introductory way, the instruction was:

'When you come into a town and they make you welcome, eat the food provided for you; heal the sick there, and say: "The kingdom of God has come close to you!" '

When He got into an argument about casting out devils by Beelzebub the prince of devils, He said: 'But if it is by the finger of God that I drive out the devils, then be sure the kingdom of God has already come upon you.'

Jesus Himself was the instrument of this new here-and-nowness of the kingdom of God. He made this much plain from the start, but left His hearers to pick up for themselves the—to them—staggering implication of it: that He was himself Messiah. As Messiah, therefore, He was fulfilling in His own person the 'future' kingdom of God of Old Testament thinking, yet in a way so different from the traditional picture that for a long time few recognized it. His view of Messiahship was of the suffering servant pictured by the second Isaiah (Isaiah 53) rather than the ruling prince of the earlier prophet (Isaiah 11) and other Old Testament prophets. Inevitably, therefore, the kingdom of God was not yet established on earth in the sense that Isaiah 11 foresaw it. This still remained in the future.

In the second sense, Jesus represented the kingdom of God as a future eternal community and referred to it in all sorts of different guises—'the world to come', a feast to which Gentiles would be invited, a 'kingdom prepared for you from the foundation of the world', and so on. But before this could come about the here-and-now kingdom of God must be made known and experienced all the world over. Messiah must first suffer and die in the spirit of Isaiah 53 before preparations for the final consummation of God's purpose in the eternal community of God could begin.

It is not clear in some of the Gospel references whether Jesus was referring to the present or the future 'kingdom'. One thing is clear, however, that entering the kingdom of God—both now and hereafter—is the prize worth striving for above everything else, the pearl without price, the treasure worth selling everything to buy, the thing we should 'seek first' and stop worrying about less important matters. But, as all these references imply, there is a price to pay, which may be a very high one. Only the right kind of people can enter the kingdom, and Jesus mentioned quite a few relevant qualifications:

Repentance—Mark 1: 15; Luke 13: 3; 15: 18; 19: 9. This seems to imply not merely being sorry for sins, but making a break with the past and changing one's whole approach to life.

Humility—Matthew 5: 3; Luke 18: 13.

Childlikeness—Mark 10: 15. Perhaps especially this meant implicit, unquestioning trust in God.

Goodness, or keeping the commandments—Matthew 5: 20; 7: 21; 19: 17.

Sacrifice—Matthew 5: 10; 16: 24; Luke 18: 29.

Helpfulness—Luke 10: 28; Matthew 25: 34.

Interestingly, faith is not specifically mentioned as a qualification for the kingdom of God, though obviously in a sense it is taken for granted all through; no one can enter God's sphere of influence until he believes in it. But the Jesus of the synoptic Gospels did not preach anything approaching the idea that 'we are saved by faith alone'; quite the contrary.

One would not suggest, of course, that the qualifications listed above are in the nature of separate, obligatory tests like passing a series of examinations. That would be to misunderstand the whole spirit and method of Jesus' teaching. Rather they are to be regarded as illustrations of the kind of change of heart and mind—described so vividly in Matthew's version of the Sermon on the Mount—which is the essential prerequisite for sharing in the glorious treasure of God's presence and power. Indeed, running through all this teaching is the strong implication that anyone who sincerely and earnestly seeks to serve God in the spirit of the Sermon on the Mount will be rewarded with 'the kingdom':

'Ask, and you will receive; seek, and you will find; knock, and the door will be opened.'

'Have no fear, little flock; for your Father has chosen to give you the Kingdom.'

Yet 'The gate that leads to life is small and the road is narrow, and those who find it are few'—and the implication is that the many failed to find it because they were asking in the wrong way, seeking the wrong things and knocking on the wrong doors.

THE NEW WINE

The message of Jesus was revolutionary not only in its sense of crisis—'You did not recognize God's moment when it came'—but also in the sharp conflict it provoked with the authorities of religious tradition and social convention. This was brought out very early in His ministry and in Mark 2 and 3 we have five separate incidents illustrating this conflict on three different issues. The champions of the establishment were the Scribes ('lawyers' in the N.E.B.) and the Pharisees, who in their different ways were concerned to defend the general principles of law and the defined standards of ritual morality.

The first issue was the Sin Barrier. When Jesus presumed to offer forgiveness to the paralytic who had been brought to Him for healing, the lawyers objected that only God could forgive sins. One suspects that they objected not only because Jesus' forgiveness was unauthorized—i.e., not done through the proper channels—but perhaps even more because it was offered free—without the need for any sin-offering or ritual observance to put things right with the Law and without the intermediation of a priest. Again, it was doctors of the law who objected when Jesus associated with tax-gatherers and other bad characters. Society seemed to be divided fairly sharply into respectable people and Sinners, and the Sinners were beyond the pale of decent social intercourse. Jesus with His new gospel broke the Sin Barrier not only by offering forgiveness free, but by making friends with those who should be kept beyond the pale. How could the Law be upheld if people in positions of authority condoned sin by hobnobbing with recognized and unrepentant sinners?

The second issue was fasting. Here Jesus passed off the criticism by talking about the bridegroom and his friends, but the implication was that he and his disciples were not subject to the accepted rules of ritual fasting.

The third issue was Sabbath observance. While we might have objected that the disciples were stealing someone else's corn, the Pharisees objected that they were working on the Sabbath. Again, Jesus claimed not to be subject to the restrictions which had been laid down by tradition.

All these incidents illustrate the idea of freedom. It may well be that Jesus brought them about deliberately to emphasize the inherent conflict with tradition. Be that as it may, He summed them up in the parables of the patched coat and the new wine. The new wine of His gospel was too explosive to be contained in the old wine-skins of legalism and restrictionism.

This emphasis on the 'newness' of the gospel and its freedom from outward restrictions is in line with the 'new covenant' of Jeremiah 31:

'Behold, the days are coming, says the Lord, when I will

make a new covenant with the house of Israel and the house of Judah . . .

'But this is the covenant which I will make with the house of Israel after those days, says the Lord: I will put my law within them, and I will write it upon their hearts; and I will be their God and they shall be my people.'

To enter the here-and-now kingdom of God was to have God's law within: to be freed from the outward compulsion of 'The Law' with its laid down observances of sin-offerings and fasting and Sabbath rules, but to be bound by the inner compulsion of God's grace; and this, as the Sermon on the Mount showed only too clearly, meant a higher standard, not a lower.

THE UPSIDE-DOWN VALUES

To enter the kingdom of music you must have an ear for it. To enter the kingdom of art you must have the vision. To enter the here-and-now kingdom of God you need a new scale of values. This is the message of the beatitudes, and the very first line declared bluntly that the values were disconcertingly different from commonly accepted ones:

'How blest are those who know that they are poor; the kingdom of Heaven is theirs.'

H. G. Wells had a short story about a man who could work miracles. He discovered this aptitude because one day, by way of demonstration, he turned a paraffin lamp upside-down, and it went on burning. It was part of the miracle of the here-and-now kingdom of God as Jesus taught it that it turned commonly accepted values and standards upside down. The inversion is summarized in the first and later parts of the Sermon on the Mount and re-emphasized again and again in subsequent teaching and actions of Jesus. A man who has found the glorious treasure of this kingdom is an odd character by normal standards if we are to take Christ's teaching seriously.

In the first place, he will not want to be rich:

'Do not store up for yourselves treasure on earth, where it

grows rusty and moth-eaten, and thieves break in to steal it . . . You cannot serve God and Money.' (Matthew 6: 19)

'Set your mind on God's kingdom and his justice before everything else, and all the rest will come to you as well.' (Matthew 6: 33)

'Be on your guard against greed of every kind, for even when a man has more than enough, his wealth does not give him life.' (Luke 12: 15)

'It is easier for a camel to pass through the eye of a needle than for a rich man to enter the kingdom of God.' (Mark 10; 25)

In the second place, he will not want to be important, in the usual sense of the word:

'How blest are those of a gentle spirit; they shall have the earth for their possession.' (Matthew 5: 5)

'Everyone who exalts himself will be humbled; and whoever humbles himself will be exalted.' (Matthew 23: 12; Luke 14: 11; 18: 14)

'You know that in the world, rulers lord it over their subjects, and their great men make them feel the weight of authority; but it shall not be so with you. Among you, whoever wants to be great must be your servant and whoever would be first must be the willing slave of all.' (Matthew 20: 25)

In the third place, he will not want to get his own back:

'How blest are the peacemakers; God shall call them his sons.' (Matthew 5: 9)

'You have learned that they were told, "An eye for an eye and a tooth for a tooth." But what I tell you is this: Do not set yourself against the man who wrongs you.' (Matthew 5: 38)

'For if you forgive others the wrongs they have done, your heavenly Father will also forgive you; but if you do not forgive others, then the wrongs you have done will not be forgiven by your Father.' (Matthew 6: 14)

'. . . Jesus replied, "I do not say seven times; I say seventy times seven." ' (Matthew 18: 22)

The upside-down values of the kingdom were part of the reason for its revolutionary impact: part of the explosiveness of the new wine which could not be contained in the old wine-skins of the establishment.

THE NEW MORALITY

Very early in His ministry Jesus was accused of breaking the Law. Indeed, to the legal minded He seemed to be playing fast and loose with the Law and the traditional standards of conduct which were part of the Law. It was necessary, therefore, for Him to make His position quite clear, and this He did in the Sermon on the Mount, as an introduction to His outline of the 'new morality' of the here-and-now kingdom of God:

'Do not suppose that I have come to abolish the Law and the prophets; I did not come to abolish, but to complete.'

It soon became apparent that the new morality—as Jeremiah foresaw—was different in kind from the old morality of the Law; but its first impact in the Sermon on the Mount was one of degree: it went much further than the requirements of the Law and demanded a much higher standard; 'Unless you show yourselves far better men than the Pharisees and the doctors of the law, you can never enter the kingdom of Heaven.' In a sense, therefore, the Sermon on the Mount was a counterblast to the lawyers' accusations of breaking the Law. The standards he demanded were 'impossible' standards; they are only credible in the light of the new values and attitude to life already outlined in the beatitudes.

In part 1 of the sermon, then, Jesus indicated the new scale of values of the kingdom; in part 2 He illustrated the new moral standards which arose out of that scale of values and could only make sense if based upon it; and in part 3 gave some examples of the change in personal relationships which it involved—though the three parts overlap to some extent.

Part 2 is concerned with moral standards in matters of straightforward, easily definable personal conduct, as laid down in the Ten Commandments, and in each case Jesus went a big step further than the original requirement—not to abolish the Law, but to 'complete' it:

'You have learned that our forefathers were told, "Do not commit murder; anyone who commits murder must be brought to judgement." But what I tell you is this . . .'

'You have learned that they were told, "Do not commit adultery." But what I tell you is this . . .'

'They were told, "A man who divorces his wife must give her a note of dismissal." But what I tell you is this . . .'

'Again, you have learned that they were told, "Do not break your oath." But what I tell you is this . . .'

Part 3 is concerned with personal relationships and attitudes, and could be considered a further extension of moral standards into those regions where actions are less easily defined. But the principle is the same—the requirements of the kingdom of God go far beyond those of established tradition, and only make sense if they are part of, and gain their inspiration from, the new values outlined in Part 1:

'You have learned that they were told, "An eye for an eye and a tooth for a tooth." But what I tell you is this . . .'

'You have learned that they were told, "Love your neighbour, hate your enemy." But what I tell you is this . . .'

'Be careful not to make a show of your religion before men . . .' (Then follow examples of giving in charity, prayer and fasting.)

'Pass no judgement, and you will not be judged. For as you judge others, so you will yourselves be judged.'

The whole Sermon, then, can be seen as part of the step-by-step development of the teaching of Christ, whether it was actually delivered all in one piece, as in Matthew, or in two or more parts at different times, as in Luke.

THE POWER OF FAITH

After the Sermon on the Mount, in both Matthew's and Luke's order of events, the healing ministry continues with a special emphasis on the power of faith. This is a theme which is strangely absent from the Sermon itself, though strongly emphasized on other occasions. As we have seen, the early proclamation of the kingdom was closely identified with healing miracles, as if power-for-good were the main evidence that the kingdom was here-and-now. After the sophisticated discourses in the Sermon on the values, attitudes and demands of the kingdom, the healing miracles go on, but with repeated emphasis that power-for-good depends on faith. If it is not stretching the point too far, one can regard this theme as an addendum to the Sermon itself. It seems to mean that sufferers who had faith in Christ could reap some of the benefits of the kingdom without actually entering into it, or indeed knowing anything about it; it may mean also that those who had really entered into the true meaning of the kingdom had healing power themselves—as the disciples did later—because they were so close to God that His power was available to them; the faith needed to heal was certainly of a different order from the faith needed to be healed, but the distinction is not clear in the Gospels.

It should be emphasized, however, that this theme of faith had nothing to do with belief in any set of doctrines, or with spiritual salvation or eternal life. It was concerned with getting things done; on the one hand the faith in Christ which enabled Him to bring healing to those who had it; on the other hand the faith in God's power which enabled Him, and later His disciples, to use that power:

'Your faith is too weak. I tell you this: if you have faith no bigger even than a mustard seed, you will say to this mountain, "Move from here to there!", and it will move; nothing will be impossible for you.' (Matthew 17: 20)

'I tell you this: if only you have faith and have no doubts, you will do what has been done to the fig tree; and more than that, you need only say to this mountain, "Be lifted from your place and hurled into the sea", and what you say will be done.' (Matthew 21: 21)

Even if I am right in regarding the power-of-faith theme as an addendum to the Sermon on the Mount, it is certainly not specifically connected therewith, and throughout the teaching of the synoptic Gospels the business of physically getting things done through faith is strangely separate from and unconnected with the theme of the kingdom of God and eternal life or spiritual 'salvation'.

THE LAW WITHIN

We have seen how the early teaching of Christ is developed in logical sequence in the synoptic accounts, something like this:

1. Simple proclamation that the kingdom of God, demonstrated by power-for-good, is here, now.
2. Demonstrations of the conflict between this and the tradition, showing that the new gospel cannot be contained in the old mould.
3. Explanation of the new scale of values and the new standards of morality and personal relationships which the gospel of the kingdom requires.
4. (Rather off at a tangent): Emphasis on the power of faith to do good.

The next step in this sequence is the teaching on how the kingdom 'grows', but before dealing with this we shall interrupt the chronological sequence in order to insert an idea which is borrowed from the subsequent teaching of Jesus and which forms a useful link at this stage in the logical development. It is only present by implication in the Sermon on the Mount, but is brought out clearly later in the synoptic Gospels. It is closely akin to the theme of Jeremiah 31: 31 already quoted. While Jeremiah spoke of God's law within, Jesus taught that God's rule was here-and-now and invited people to 'enter into it'. Both seem to mean exactly the same thing.

Jeremiah's famous text was linked in the preceding two verses with the idea of individual responsibility:

'In those days they shall no longer say, "The fathers have eaten sour grapes, and the children's teeth are set on edge." But everyone shall die for his own sin; each man who eats sour grapes, his teeth shall be set on edge.'

The new moral law he envisaged was not a communal law, established for the community by God and imposed by the community on the individual; it was the inner light of individual conscience, lit by the grace of God and maintaining the kind of standards which cannot be imposed from without—'For they shall all know me, from the least of them to the greatest, says the Lord.' To have this law within was to accept a trust from God, to be on one's honour to do right, or to use the Pauline idiom, to be 'under grace' instead of under the law.

The new morality of Jesus was likewise a morality oı inner standards. He claimed freedom from many of the outward restrictions imposed by tradition, but at the same time demanded a much higher standard of inner integrity, of a kind which no amount of rules and regulations could impose. This was the 'completing' of the law, and in later teaching Jesus emphasized on several occasions that it is the inward things that matter rather than the outward:

'You Pharisees! You clean the outside of cup and plate; but inside you there is nothing but greed and wickedness. You fools! Did not he who made the outside make the inside too?' (Luke 11: 39)

'Alas for you Pharisees! You pay tithes of mint and rue and every garden-herb, but have no care for justice and the love of God.' (11: 42)

'Nothing that goes into a man from outside can defile him; no, it is the things that come out of him that defile a man.' (Mark 7: 15)

'You are like tombs covered with whitewash; they look well from outside, but inside they are full of dead men's bones and all kinds of filth.' (Matthew 23: 27)

A trust, once fully accepted, can be a far harder task-master than an outwardly imposed discipline. When the 'law within' has become part of oneself there is no escaping from it, no evasion, no covering up. So the new morality of Jesus, because its inspiration was from within, was different in kind from the formal morality of the Law; and the difference in degree—'But what I tell you is this . . .' —was only possible because of this difference in kind.

THE PROPAGATION OF THE GOSPEL

We return now to the chronological sequence. The Good News Jesus preached, in its early simplest form, was this:

The kingdom of God is not God's rule imposed on nations from His throne in heaven; it is here and now, for you.

Since the kingdom is within, therefore, it is not to be established by the power of nations and their armies, nor by the just rule of princes (as in Isaiah 11), nor propagated by priestly edict or by rules and regulations imposed by law. It is propagated from person to person and grows silently, like seed in fruitful soil.

This was the next theme in the synoptic teachings and we find it in Matthew 13, Mark 4 and Luke 8. To us who are familiar with it the meaning is obvious enough and needs no reiteration, but it was evidently necessary for Jesus to repeat it almost ad nauseam to drive the point home, and even then the implication is that only the intimate disciples understood, while to the crowd it was a string of somewhat mystifying parables.

Taking material from the three Gospels and using the order of Mark, the section began with the parable of the sower, in which the seed is the word of the kingdom. Then followed the parables of the lamp, the seed which grows while man sleeps, the good seed and the darnel, the mustard seed, and the yeast—with other parables of the kingdom having somewhat different lessons. Some little time later Jesus commissioned the twelve to be sowers of the seed themselves, thus confirming the truth of the theme in their own experience. At this stage they did little more than call for repentance and proclaim the kingdom, and the most important impact of the mission was probably on themselves rather than on the villages they visited. They had entered into the secret of the kingdom and found themselves part of the process of propagation. The seed which was the word of the kingdom was being spread through them.

THE SON OF MAN MUST SUFFER

The next step in the synoptic teaching, one which signalled the turning point of the campaign, was the twofold message about Jesus Himself, reserved at this stage for the intimate disciples and so staggering in its implications that even they seemed unable to accept it. That He was Himself Messiah was something they were now ready to guess. That as Messiah He would be killed, and that very soon, not only swept away all their preconceived ideas of what Messiah would do but also seemed to imply that they would be left alone to carry on the work. With the mission of the twelve they had, so to speak, passed the first test of apostleship, but they were not ready for anything like this, and the following weeks and months for them must have been an agony of fear and bewilderment.

FILLING IN THE PICTURE

During the long months of the pilgrimage to Jerusalem, Jesus added to the teaching already given, but in the synoptic records there is no obvious logical sequence here. Rather the teachings are given in response to particular questions or situations as they arise, and throughout the period there is a strong sense of urgency culminating in the dire warnings of sufferings to come. The salient passages were quoted in Chapter 8, and I will merely mention them here without comment, not because they are unimportant, but because it seems unnecessary to add anything to what has been quoted:

1. The Great Commandments and the parable of the Good Samaritan.
2. The lesson in prayer.
3. The condemnation of formalism.
4. God's care for sinners: the parable of the Two Sons.
5. Some qualifications for the kingdom.
6. The public claim to be Messiah.

THE LAST THINGS

On several earlier occasions recorded in the Gospels Jesus had touched upon the future of the world and the kingdom, but in the last few days before His death this theme seemed uppermost in His mind, and He dwelt on it at considerable length and with a great sense of urgency.

In a sense it is the last step in the logical development of the teaching in the synoptic Gospels. According to the records what Jesus said was plain and unmistakable and can be summed up thus:

There will be wars, natural disasters, persecutions and unprecedented sufferings;

Jerusalem will be attacked and completely destroyed;

Before the end the Gospel of the kingdom will be preached throughout the world;

When the time comes there will be supernatural signs and portents and the Son of Man will come in great power and glory;

The dead will be raised and the Son of Man will judge all men; the good will be received into God's eternal kingdom, the wicked consigned to eternal punishment, and the natural order of things will come to an end.

The coming of the Son of Man will be without warning, but all these things will take place soon, within the lifetime of some of those present.

On other occasions Jesus had clearly taught that the dead would be raised, and the Gospel record implies but does not state that the resurrection would take place at the time of the coming of the Son of Man—that He would judge both 'the quick and the dead'; this was Paul's interpretation—at least as far as the Christian dead were concerned—in 1 Thessalonians 4: 15-17:

'We who are left alive until the Lord comes shall not forestall those who have died; because at the word of command, at the sound of the archangel's voice and God's trumpet-call, the Lord himself will descend from heaven; first the Christian dead will rise; then we who are left alive shall join them, caught up in the clouds to meet the Lord in the air.'

Although what Jesus said is plain enough, what He meant by it could be interpreted in various ways. He used apocalyptic images and modes of expression which were current at the time but may be incomprehensible to us. Did He expect the stars literally to fall from the sky, the Son of Man to come literally in a cloud and send out teams of angels to collect people who had risen literally from their graves, and transport them into the eternal kingdom? Or, at the other extreme of interpretation, were all these figures of speech and did He envisage a 'spiritual' second coming into the lives of the apostles as at Pentecost, calling the righteous through the preaching of the Church and receiving the souls of the redeemed into eternal life? From my own reading of the Gospels but with very little background knowledge my impression is that He thought of cataclysmic events and a spectacular coming of the Son of Man in a fairly literal sense; but that His thoughts and the images in which He expressed them were influenced by extreme mental and spiritual strain—being to some extent the product of his own situation as well as being expressed in the current images of his time. It is perhaps worth noting that in His resurrection appearances the sense of extreme urgency and approaching cataclysm was no longer present.

Whatever the correct interpretation of Christ's teaching on the last things, one thing is not subject to doubt: He stated categorically that the events He prophesied would take place soon. Though the form of the events might be interpreted in various ways, the timing was made abundantly and emphatically clear.

In several discourses, illustrated by such parables as the householder and the thief, the servants whose master was away, and the wise and foolish virgins, He drove home the lesson that the things He described would happen to them, His hearers—He was speaking to His disciples, not the crowd—and they were to await the end with tense expectation as something within their own personal experience. One does not speak in such terms of events which are to be delayed for two thousand years or more—about as long as the total history of the Hebrews from Abraham to Christ.

This overwhelming sense of urgency is in itself sufficient evidence that Jesus was speaking literally of the near future, but apart from this He stated as much quite specifically in three sayings on different occasions reported slightly differently in the different Gospels—referring not only to imminent wars and the destruction of Jerusalem, but to God's final consummation, described in Matthew 13 as 'the end of time':

'When you are persecuted in one town, take refuge in another; I tell you this: before you have gone through all the towns of Israel the Son of Man will have come.' (Matthew 10: 23. This saying is associated with the first mission of the twelve, but warnings of persecution in the same passage clearly look forward to a later period; it is so similar to sayings recorded just before Christ's death that the passage may well be misplaced here.)

'If anyone is ashamed of me and mine in this wicked and godless age, the Son of Man will be ashamed of him, when he comes in the glory of his Father and the holy angels.' He also said, 'I tell you this: there are some of those standing here who will not taste death before they have seen the kingdom of God already come in power.' (Mark 8: 38; also Matthew 16: 27)

'Then they will see the Son of Man coming in the clouds with great power and glory. . . . I tell you this: the present generation will live to see it all. Heaven and earth will pass away; my words will never pass away.' (Mark 13: 26, 30; also Matthew 24: 34 and Luke 21: 32)

The apostles evidently interpreted His prophecies in this immediate sense. In the passage quoted above from 1 Thessalonians—the earliest of Paul's letters that we have—the apostle clearly expected to be still alive at the resurrection, when the Lord comes; while Peter, in 1 Peter 4: 7, enjoined prayer and sobriety because 'The end of all things is upon us.'

The down to earth parts of Christ's prophecies were indeed fulfilled soon enough, in the terrible destruction of Jerusalem and scattering of the Jews in A.D. 70, when 'the abomination of desolation' (the Roman standard) did enter the Temple; and the gospel was indeed 'proclaimed to all nations' of the then known world. But if He meant that the angels would come literally to gather the chosen, and if He meant the coming of the Son of Man 'like lightning from the east, flashing as far as the west' in any sense more literal than a coming of His spirit in the spectacular expansion of the early Church, then events proved Him to be wrong. These things did not take place.

There seems, therefore, to be little justification for repeating nineteen centuries later, as an article of faith capable of being postponed into a still more distant future, that 'From thence he shall come to judge the quick and the dead.'

LIFE AFTER DEATH

How does the life after death of Christians fit into Christ's teaching on the Last Things? Jesus certainly taught that there is life after death, but on this theme the synoptic Gospels contain at least two different strands of thought which do not meet. Early Old Testament ideas on the subject thought of a shadowy, purposeless existence of disembodied spirits in Sheol, the abode of shades, but later writers pictured a great future consummation of God's purpose when the dead would rise from their graves. Thus:

Isaiah 26: 19—

Thy dead shall live, their bodies shall rise.
O dwellers in the dust, awake and sing for joy!
For thy dew is a dew of light,
And on the land of the shades thou wilt let it fall.

The writer of Daniel connected this future resurrection with a time of judgement:

'At that time shall arise Michael, the great prince who has charge of your people. And there shall be a time of trouble, such as never has been since there was a nation till that time; but at that time your people shall be delivered, every one whose name shall be found written in the book. And many of those who sleep in the dust of the earth shall awake, some to everlasting life, and some to shame and everlasting contempt.' (Daniel 12: 1)

Jesus was clearly very much influenced by the book of Daniel, and much of his imagery of resurrection, judgement and the coming of the Son of Man is taken therefrom.

It was apparently this Old Testament concept of bodily resurrection, not immediately after death but at the end of the age, which was current at the time of Jesus though not accepted by everyone; and Jesus did not seem to contradict it:

'. . . At the resurrection whose wife is she to be, since all seven had married her?' Jesus said to them, 'The men and women of this world marry; but those who have been judged worthy of a place in the other world and of the resurrection from the dead, do not marry, for they are not subject to death any longer. They are like angels; they are sons of God, because they share in the resurrection.' (Luke 20: 33)

The apostles and the early Church clearly accepted this

view of the resurrection and regarded the bodily resurrection of Christ as an earnest of the future bodily resurrection of the Christian dead, at the end of the age.

On the other hand, some of Christ's teaching about eternal life and the kingdom of God clearly implied that good people do not have to wait for a future world-wide consummation—'The Resurrection' and 'The Judgement'—before they enter into God's eternal kingdom; that being in the kingdom of God is here-and-now, and eternal life is the continuing of that experience after death:

Matthew 5: 12. 'Accept it with gladness and exultation, for you have a rich reward in heaven.'

Matthew 6: 1. 'Be careful not to make a show of your religion before men; if you do, no reward awaits you in your Father's house in heaven.'

Luke 16: 22. 'One day the poor man died and was carried away by the angels to be with Abraham. The rich man also died and was buried, and in Hades, where he was in torment, he looked up; and there, far away, was Abraham with Lazarus close beside him.'

Luke 23: 43. 'I tell you this: today you shall be with me in Paradise.'

Mark 12: 26. 'Now about the resurrection of the dead, have you never read in the Book of Moses, in the story of the burning bush, how God spoke to him and said, "I am the God of Abraham, the God of Isaac, and the God of Jacob"? God is not God of the dead, but of the living.'

This last passage, like the story of the transfiguration, clearly implies that Jesus thought of these saints of old as already enjoying an eternal life which was of the spirit—not having to await a bodily resurrection at the end of the age—and He adduced their present immortality as evidence 'that the dead are raised to life again'.

In view of these differing strands of thought in the Gospels it is not surprising that the Church's teaching on life after death is sometimes vague. Roman Catholic doctrine overcomes the problem by simply adding the strands together and inserting two extra bits not found in the Gospels, in order to make a coherent whole, which might be summarized thus:

We are both body and spirit. At death our spirit goes either to Heaven, to Purgatory or to Hell. At the end of the world the bodily resurrection will take place and then the body will be re-united with the soul. Because there are alternative destinations for the spirit, there must be a judgement of each individual immediately after death, and this is called the 'Particular Judgement' as distinct from the 'Final Judgement'—a world event which takes place on the last day.

It seems to me highly artificial and naive thus to synthesize the two ideas: the one of bodily resurrection at the last day, the other a spiritual concept of being in the presence of God here and now, and entering His eternal presence at death. The two seem to me to be alternative expressions of the same spiritual truth: the former a primitive Hebrew image apparently accepted by the early Church; the latter a more sophisticated interpretation which seems to be implicit though not emphasized in much of the teaching of Christ.

Be that as it may, the meaning of Christ's teaching on the subject seems to me to be still a matter of doubt. Suffice to say that He did emphatically teach that death is not the end; and that those who are accounted worthy may enter into God's living presence now and into His eternal presence hereafter.

JUDGEMENT, HEAVEN AND HELL

There is another and more serious apparent contradiction in the synoptic teaching of life after death, and it concerns the theme of judgement. In the teaching of Jesus, Heaven and Hell were very real and very important and there is no escaping from them. According to the Gospels—especially

Matthew's—He warned people of the prospect of eternal punishment with a solemnity and urgency which brooks no dilution, and this seems to stand in direct contrast to His assurance of God's loving care.

There is one possible way out of the contradiction. Jesus spoke of Satan or the Devil in a way which was presumably current at the time, and which could probably be interpreted either in terms of a single, personal 'Prince of Evil' or in terms of a convenient personification of the power of evil in the world. If the first interpretation is correct and he regarded Satan as 'a person', acting independently of God and against God's will, then this could provide a rational solution to the contradiction between the eternal punishment of Hell and the loving care of God. This approach does seem to be hinted at in some of His teachings in the synoptic Gospels:

Matthew 4: 10. But Jesus said, 'Begone, Satan; Scripture says, "You shall do homage to the Lord your God and worship him alone." '

Matthew 12 : 26. '. . . And if it is Satan who casts out Satan, Satan is divided against himself; how then can his kingdom stand?'

Luke 12: 4. 'Do not fear those who kill the body and after that have nothing more they can do . . . fear him who, after he has killed, has authority to cast into hell. Believe me, he is the one to fear. Are not sparrows five for twopence? And yet not one of them is overlooked by God. More than that, even the hairs of your head have all been counted. Have no fear; you are worth more than any number of sparrows.'

These strongly suggest that Satan acts against God's will, gains a hold over men's lives, and when they die drags them down to his own level—'the eternal fire that is ready for the devil and his angels.' The close linking of this warning of hell with one of the most telling descriptions of God's loving care for the individual suggests that if we allow ourselves to fall into the grip of Satan, God is powerless to rescue us from him who 'has authority to cast into hell'.

Unfortunately this explanation will not stand up against the emphatic and oft-repeated picture of the Judgement in which it is not Satan but God, or the Son of Man acting on God's behalf, who consigns the wicked to eternal punishment:

'But it will be more bearable, I tell you, for the land of Sodom on the day of judgement than for you.'

'. . . As the darnel, then, is gathered up and burnt, so at the end of time the Son of Man will send out his angels, who will gather out of his kingdom everything that causes offence, and all whose deeds are evil, and these will be thrown into the blazing furnace, the place of wailing and grinding of teeth.'

'Again the kingdom of Heaven is like a net let down into the sea, where fish of every kind were caught in it . . . That is how it will be at the end of time. The angels will go forth, and they will separate the wicked from the good, and throw them into the blazing furnace, the place of wailing and grinding of teeth.'

'. . . it is better to enter into life with one eye than to keep both eyes and be thrown into the fires of hell.' (Matthew 11: 24; 13: 40, 47, 49; 18: 9)

The Church has tried to cover up the contradiction by speaking of the 'justice' of God as something not incompatible with His love, but this simply will not do. It is certainly neither loving nor just to consign anyone to eternal torment as a punishment for finite sins committed in a finite lifetime; still less so if the sins are regarded as a result of failing to resist the machinations of a cunning and powerful Devil, and still less again in the borderline case of the man who genuinely tries to keep to the straight and narrow way but just fails to make the grade.

The Catholic Church softens the harshness of Judgement with the convenient theory of Purgatory, where those who fail to make the grade are given a second chance—a reasonable idea but not to be found in the New Testament.

Another way of re-interpreting the Judgement is to say that Heaven is being with God and Hell is the agony of being away from Him; but the picture of eternal punishment in the Gospels is much more positive than that.

Yet another attempt to rationalize the theme is to regard Hell as the inevitable consequence of disobeying moral laws which, being part of the God-given order of things, cannot be flouted with impunity—just as flouting natural laws can have dire and inevitable consequences. This seems to me to be a sensible approach, and I would regard it as reasonable to suppose that the nature of our life after death will be dependent, for good or ill, upon the way we live our life here and now. But it has little in common with the Judgement of the Gospels, in which Hell is emphatically not an unfortunate consequence but a punishment, meted out ruthlessly with no appeal and no allowance for borderline cases.

As I see it the two ideas are quite incompatible. The concept of a Judgement under God, in which those who do not find favour are consigned to eternal punishment, whether one interprets it literally or figuratively, simply cannot be reconciled with the theme of God's forgiving love for all men and especially for the sinner.

It may well be that Jesus did not actually use this picture of the Judgement; in its uncompromising form it is only found in Matthew's Gospel, where it is repeated several times, and these passages may therefore represent other traditions wrongly ascribed to Christ. But if He really did teach this theme, the only explanation I can think of is that He was using the prevailing idiom of judgement and Hell, although in that form it flagrantly contradicted His teaching on the love of God, in order to emphasize dramatically the urgency of decision and the supreme contrast between the joy of entering the kingdom of God and the misery of being left out of it. I do not find this a very satisfactory explanation, but if it is true the judgement sayings are to be placed in almost the same category as hyperbolic expressions such as 'If it is your eye that is your undoing, tear it out and fling it away'—an injunction which no one dreamt of taking literally, and which was followed by a reference, perhaps equally hyperbolic, to the fires of hell. To the thinking of Christ's day the judgement image was familiar and evidently presented no contradiction, but to present-day thinking it does, and for us today to present Matthew's version of judgement and hell as part of Christian theology makes nonsense of the whole.

10 The Interpretation of John

BEFORE attempting to summarize the message of the fourth Gospel it is necessary to make some general observations.

In the first place, as we have already seen, this Gospel has a specific purpose and the material is clearly selected and presented with this purpose in mind.

In the second place much of the message is expressed in pictorial and metaphorical terms and this, too, is frankly acknowledged. There is an obvious danger in pressing the metaphors to too literal an interpretation. It is fairly clear from the sweepingly metaphorical language that the author did not intend his figures of speech to be taken in a literal, dogmatic sense: to do so would involve quite a few direct contradictions, because in several passages statements are made which in any literal sense would contradict one another—and they are placed quite close together, as if by deliberate antithesis. For example:

1: 12. But to all who did receive him, to those who have yielded him their allegiance, he gave the right to become children of God, not born of any human stock, or by the fleshly desire of a human father, but the offspring of God himself.

1: 14. He came to dwell among us, and we saw his glory, such glory as befits the Father's only son, full of grace and truth.

5: 19. 'In truth, in very truth I tell you, the Son can do nothing by himself; he only does what he sees the Father doing.'

5: 22. 'And again, the Father does not judge anyone, but has given full jurisdiction to the Son.'

6: 40. 'For it is the Father's will that everyone who looks upon the Son and puts his faith in him shall possess eternal life.'

6: 53. 'In truth, in very truth I tell you, unless you eat the flesh of the Son of Man and drink his blood, you can have no life in you.'

In the third place, the Gospel portrays a Jesus quite different from the Jesus of the synoptics—different in His message, in His language and imagery, in His claims and in His attitude to His hearers. Jesus as Son of God is the central theme and, in complete contrast to the other Gospels, here He argues His own case, presenting Himself to the people and describing His own functions as saviour and mediator. In the synoptics it is the kingdom of God which He presents to the people: while cryptic Messianic claims do seem to slip in at an early stage, they are not comprehended by the people, and He only claims openly to be Messiah a few days before His death, even then obliquely, by symbolically fulfilling a well-known prophecy.

In the fourth place, this Gospel, after a brief philosophical introduction and unlike the other three, plunges straight into deep theology. Here there is no sense of stage-by-stage development of Christ's teaching through the course of His ministry—it is the full message more or less from the start.

Some of the incidents in this Gospel are so vividly described that they have all the marks of personal, eye-witness recollections; yet even an eye-witness account is subject to considerable error if it is written down sixty years or more after the event. Throughout the Gospel the incidents, discourses and arguments are inextricably interwoven, so that sometimes it is difficult to tell where the discourse of Jesus ends and the explanation by the author begins, they are so much all of a piece.

All these considerations, it seems to me, add up to a fairly definite conclusion. The book was probably written with full knowledge of existing accounts of the ministry of Jesus, and some of its incidents were probably included to supplement the earlier accounts or fill in the gaps. But this is not the primary purpose of it. It is not a history of the life and teaching of Jesus, but a treatise on theology—the theology of the author; and the theology is knitted into the framework provided by the ministry of Jesus. As such it is to be treated with all the respect due to one of the two great theologians of the early Church, but it cannot be taken as an alternative account of the teaching of Christ. To an unbiased layman studying the four Gospels, and assuming that herein lie the best available records of events, there seems to me to be only one reasonable conclusion: that the first three Gospels collectively provide a sketchy and imperfect, but basically accurate account of what Jesus actually did and said, while the fourth provides an interpretation of these events by one man, whom we may call John even though there is doubt about his identity. That is why I have called it 'The interpretation of John'.

Because the discourses and arguments are so obviously rendered in the author's own language and idiom, I would think it impossible even for the experts to say how much of the teaching recorded in this Gospel is likely to have been, in fact, the teaching of Jesus, and how much was that of the author, put into the mouth of Jesus. Therefore, we are not in a position even to use this teaching to supplement that of the other Gospels in order to provide a fuller record of what Jesus actually taught. We must value the material as representing the faith of a man who was a deep thinker and a dedicated disciple, who had been, at the least, very close to the events himself and was probably an eye-witness of them and participant in them.

I shall therefore attempt to summarize the message of the fourth Gospel, in the words of the New English Bible—not as a supplement to the preceding chapters on the synoptic Gospels, but as an interpretation.

Introduction: The Word made Flesh

When all things began, the Word already was. The Word dwelt with God, and what God was, the Word was. The Word, then, was with God at the beginning, and through him all things came to be; no single thing was created without him. All that came to be was alive with his life, and that life was the light of men. The light shines on in the dark, and the darkness has never quenched it.

He was in the world; but the world, though it owed its being to him, did not recognize him. He entered his own realm, and his own would not receive him. But to all who did receive him, to those who have yielded him their allegiance, he gave the right to become children of God, not born of any human stock, or by the fleshly desire of a human father, but the offspring of God himself. So the Word became flesh; he came to dwell among us, and we saw his glory, such glory as befits the Father's only Son, full of grace and truth.

Out of his full store we have all received grace upon grace; for while the Law was given through Moses, grace and truth came through Jesus Christ. No one has ever seen God; but God's only Son, he who is nearest to the Father's heart, he has made him known. (John 1: 1-5, 10-14, 16-18)

The life of the spirit

Jesus answered, 'In truth I tell you, no one can enter the kingdom of God without being born from water and spirit. Flesh can give birth only to flesh; it is spirit that gives birth to spirit. You ought not to be astonished, then, when I tell you that you must be born again. The wind blows where it wills; you hear the sound of it, but you do not know where it comes from, or where it is going. So with everyone who is born from spirit.'

'Everyone who drinks this water will be thirsty again, but whoever drinks the water that I shall give him will never suffer thirst any more. The water that I shall give him will be an inner spring always welling up for eternal life.'

'But the time approaches, indeed it is already here, when those who are real worshippers will worship the Father in spirit and in truth. Such are the worshippers whom the Father wants. God is spirit, and those who worship him must worship in spirit and in truth.' (John 3: 5-8; 4: 13-14, 23-24)

The authority and divinity of Christ

This deed in Cana-in-Galilee is the first of the signs by which Jesus revealed his glory and led his disciples to believe in him.

The woman answered, 'I know that Messiah' (that is, Christ) 'is coming. When he comes he will tell us everything.' Jesus said, 'I am he, I who am speaking to you now.'

. . . This made the Jews still more determined to kill him, because he was not only breaking the Sabbath, but, by calling God his own Father, he claimed equality with God.

To this charge Jesus replied, 'In truth, in very truth I tell you, the Son can do nothing by himself; he does only what he sees the Father doing: what the Father does, the Son does. For the Father loves the Son and shows him all his works, and will show greater yet, to fill you with wonder.

'If I testify on my own behalf, that testimony does not hold good. There is another who bears witness for me, and I know that his testimony holds. Your messengers have been to John; you have his testimony to the truth. Not that I rely on human testimony, but I remind you of it, for your own salvation. John was a lamp, burning brightly, and for a time you were ready to exult in his light. But I rely on a testimony higher than John's. There is enough to testify that the Father has sent me, in the works my Father gave me to do and to finish—the very works I have in hand. This testimony to me was given by the Father who sent me, although you never heard his voice, or saw his form. But his word has found no home in you, for you do not believe the one whom he sent. You study the scriptures diligently, supposing that in having them you have eternal life; yet, although their testimony points to me, you refuse to come to me for that life.

'If I am not acting as my Father would, do not believe me. But if I am, accept the evidence of my deeds, even if you do not believe me, so that you may recognize and know that the Father is in me, and I in the Father.'

'Anyone who has seen me has seen the Father. Then how can you say, "Show us the Father"? Do you not believe that I am in the Father and the Father in me? I am not myself the source of the words I speak to you: it is the Father who dwells in me doing his work.' (John 2: 11; 4: 25-26; 5: 18-20, 31-40; 10: 37-38; 14: 9-11)

Eternal life through faith in Christ

'God loved the world so much that he gave his only Son, that everyone who has faith in him may not die but have eternal life. It was not to judge the world that God sent his Son into the world, but that through him the world might be saved.'

'The Father loves the Son and has entrusted him with all authority. He who puts his faith in the Son has hold of eternal life, but he who disobeys the Son shall not see that life; God's wrath rests upon him.'

'For it is my Father's will that everyone who looks upon the Son and puts his faith in Him shall possess eternal life; and I will raise him up at the last day.'

'In truth, in very truth I tell you, the believer possesses eternal life.

'I am that living bread which has come down from heaven: if anyone eats this bread he shall live for ever. Moreover, the bread which I will give is my own flesh; I give it for the life of the world.' (John 3: 16-17, 35-36; 6: 40, 47, 51)

Christ the beginning

'In truth, in very truth I tell you, I am the door of the sheepfold. The sheep paid no heed to any who came before me, for they were all thieves and robbers. I am the door; anyone who comes into the fold through me shall be safe. He shall go in and out and shall find pasturage.'

'I am the way; I am truth and I am life; no one comes to the Father except by me.' (John 10: 7-9; 14: 6)

Christ the continuing

'I am the light of the world. No follower of mine shall wander in the dark; he shall have the light of life.'

'I am the real vine, and my Father is the gardener. Every barren branch of mine he cuts away; and every fruiting branch he cleans, to make it more fruitful still. You have already been cleansed by the word that I spoke to you. Dwell in me, as I in you. No branch can bear fruit by itself, but only if it remains united with the vine; no more can you bear fruit, unless you remain united with me.

'I am the vine, and you the branches. He who dwells in me, as I dwell in him, bears much fruit; for apart from me you can do nothing. He who does not dwell in me is thrown away like a withered branch. The withered branches are heaped together, thrown on the fire, and burnt.

'If you dwell in me, and my words dwell in you, ask what you will, and you shall have it. This is my Father's glory, that you may bear fruit in plenty and so be my disciples. As the Father has loved me, so I have loved you. Dwell in my love. If you heed my commands, you will dwell in my love, as I have heeded my Father's commands and dwell in his love.

'I have spoken thus to you, so that my joy may be in you, and your joy complete. This is my commandment: love one another, as I have loved you.' (John 8: 12; 15: 1-12)

Christ the end

'Set your troubled hearts at rest. Trust in God always; trust also in me. There are many dwelling-places in my Father's house; if it were not so I should have told you; for I am going there on purpose to prepare a place for you. And if I go and prepare a place for you, I shall come again and receive you to myself, so that where I am you may be also. . . . I am the way; I am the truth and I am life; no one comes to the Father except by me.'

'I am the resurrection and I am life. If a man has faith in me, even though he die, he shall come to life; and no one who is alive and has faith shall ever die.'

'Anyone who loves me will heed what I say; then my Father will love him, and we will come to him and make our dwelling with him; but he who does not love me does not heed what I say. And the word you hear is not mine: it is the word of the Father who sent me. I have told you all this while I am still here with you; but your Advocate, the Holy Spirit whom the Father will send in my name, will teach you everything, and will call to mind all that I have told you.

'Peace is my parting gift to you, my own peace, such as the world cannot give. Set your troubled hearts at rest, and banish your fears. You heard me say, "I am going away, and coming back to you." If you loved me you would have been glad to hear that I was going to the Father; for the Father is greater than I. I have told you now, beforehand, so that when it happens you may have faith.' (John 14: 1-3, 6; 11: 25-26; 14: 23-29)

Summing up

'Father, the hour has come. Glorify thy Son, that the Son may glorify thee. For thou hast made him sovereign over all mankind, to give eternal life to all whom thou hast given him. This is eternal life: to know thee who alone art truly God, and Jesus Christ whom thou hast sent.' (John 17: 1-3)

11 Translating into the Present

HAVING taken as my central theme the primary authority for Christians of Christ's teaching and example, my essay would be incomplete without some attempt to outline what that teaching is for the twentieth century. I have summarized from the Gospels what Jesus taught nineteen centuries ago—as far as a layman can from the Biblical records—but this is obviously not enough. Jesus was not speaking to the twentieth century; He was speaking to people in a different age and a different world, with a differrent culture and different ways of thought. The teaching must be 'translated' from then to now. As experts have translated His words from an ancient language to our modern one, keeping as close as possible to the original words but occasionally diverging from them where this was absolutely necessary to make them meaningful to modern ears; so we need to translate the meaning of the message from one age to another, so that the translated message will convey to our generation what the original one did to his.

This is what I have attempted to do in the last chapter—not to interpret, or to draw any conclusions, but simply to 'translate'. It is a task which bristles with difficulties and for me to attempt it is presumptuous, but I feel that the attempt must be made and the present book would be incomplete without it.

I have based the outline entirely on the synoptic Gospels, for the reasons already given—that I regard the fourth Gospel as an interpretation, in which no one can say how much, if any, of the teaching represents the actual words of Jesus; and that a synthesis of the two is ruled out because so much of the fourth Gospel, including the central theme of eternal life exclusively through faith in Christ, is completely at variance with the corresponding teaching in the synoptics.

The teaching is presented as if it were a continuous lecture. This in itself creates difficulties, but seems to be the only way of doing it. A number of important aspects of the teaching have been omitted or modified, and in order to put my cards on the table I will list the main changes which were consciously made, with the reasons for making them.

1. All reference to the principle of Messiahship is omitted. As it is found in the Gospels this is essentially related to the time and place of Christ's ministry and the fact that He and His hearers were Jews. The early apostles focused attention on Jesus Messiahsip because, again, they were speaking to Jews and their first task was to establish His unique authority. The question of the basis of Christ's authority for the twentieth century is outside the scope of this book: I have started with the proposition that if we call ourselves 'Christians' then the authority of Jesus must necessarily be paramount.

2. All reference to miracles—in the sense in which we find them in the Gospels—is also omitted.

   This seems to me to be unavoidable because we do not have the physical presence of Jesus and Christian preaching today is not, in fact, accompanied by miraculous demonstrations of the presence of the kingdom of God. The omission does, however, involve a significant modification of the teaching because Jesus linked faith very closely with healing—physical and mental healing rather than spiritual 'salvation'. Our idea of the effectiveness of faith in this day and age must be presented in a different way.

3. The expression 'kingdom of God', central though it was in the teaching of Jesus, has not been used as such. Because of associations which have become attached to

it, it tends to be either incomprehensible or very misleading. I could find no single expression to take its place and have tried to convey what I believe to be its meaning in other ways.

4. The teaching on the 'last things' has been modified in the light of actual events.

   I have omitted any reference to a spectacular second coming of Christ and the end of the world, because these ideas in the Gospels, whatever one's interpretation of their content, quite clearly referred to events to take place in the near future. They therefore cannot be transferred to our own day, many centuries later. The warning of the destruction of Jerusalem has been translated—I think legitimately—into a warning of physical destruction of the world as a whole by nuclear war, for the reason Jesus gave then: that the world is rejecting His way of peace. At the same time the teaching on judgement and Hell found particularly in Matthew's Gospel has been more or less excluded because in that form it seems to me to be in flat contradiction to the main theme of Christ's message.

5. An element has been introduced which—though commonplace in Christian thinking today—is not explicitly present in the synoptic teaching: that the Christian message is an answer to the world's problems as well as a promise of eternal life for the individual. Jesus emphatically pronounced the converse—that the world, especially Jerusalem, would suffer because of rejecting the gospel; but, unlike the prophet of Isaiah 11 : 1-9, had nothing to say about the reform of corporate national and international life through the gospel. This omission may have been an outcome of the political situation at the time, or it may have had a deeper significance.

6. An attempt has been made to break away from Bible-sounding or 'churchy' language and expressions, so that the meaning can be made clear in terms of present-day associations rather than Biblical ones; though when an expression has become part of our secular language without losing its meaning—such as 'salt of the earth'—this has been preserved, and some indispensable passages have been included in inverted commas as if quoting from the historic words of Jesus. Angels and devils have been omitted for the same kind of reason. I regard these as personifications which are not essential to the teaching and cannot, as such, be fitted into modern ways of thinking; we have different ways of expressing the same truths: for example, if the contemporaries of Jesus had known about disease microbes and been able to see them under the microscope, they would probably have called them devils.

Having outlined the main items which have been consciously changed in 'translation', it is now important to mention some of the ideas which have not been included because, as far as we know from the synoptic Gospels, Jesus did not teach them:

1. He did not teach salvation from sin through faith in Himself, though the experience of it is recorded in certain incidents, such as the conversion of Zacchaeus.
2. Nor did He suggest that salvation or eternal life in any way depends on believing in a certain set of doctrines. In particular, the doctrine of the Trinity is not explicitly mentioned in the synoptic Gospels—with the possible exception of Matthew 28: 20—and can only be derived from His teaching indirectly and by implication.
3. He gave no hint that the manner of His own birth had any special significance.

4. He never suggested that His mother had any special status, or any part to play in the spiritual life of His disciples.

5. He said nothing which could be interpreted as encouraging or permitting Christians to pray to anyone other than God, or to make use of graven images in their worship.

6. He did not lay down any formal ritual as being necessary for Christian worship, though the regular observance of 'breaking bread' from the earliest days of the Church was clearly inspired by Jesus, and became established as a ritual part of worship.

7. He gave no specific guidance on how the Christian Church should be organized.

8. He gave no inkling that communion with our heavenly Father requires the mediation of a priest, or any kind of sacrifice—not even His own.

9. Though He had much to say about His own sufferings and death, and emphasized their significance in the symbolism of breaking bread, He said nothing to suggest that a belief in the saving power of the Cross should be the central point of the Christian faith. Incidentally, this belief is not mentioned in any of the apostolic teaching recorded in Acts.

I have reiterated these points because they illustrate how some important elements in the teaching and practice of the churches do not derive from the teaching of Jesus as we know it, but have been added on to it. Two or three of the nine items listed could—with a certain amount of special pleading—be derived from sayings in the fourth Gospel, but for reasons already given I would say that even these, to the extent that they are out of keeping with the synoptic teaching, should be regarded as 'added on'.

This does not mean, of course, that Christian faith and practice should be limited to what can be found in the known teaching of Jesus. But it does mean that, provided we accept the primary authority of His teaching and example, then those elements which have been added should be regarded as expendable: if they are not in keeping with our day and age, then they may legitimately be removed; if they are seriously out of keeping with the original teaching and of no special benefit in our day and age, then they ought to be removed.

The most important 'added' elements of the apostolic faith were based on the apostles' own experience, sometimes expressed in a framework of thought derived from the Old Testament. It was clearly necessary and effective for the apostles, in their preaching, to add to the teaching of Christ their own experience of what his life, death and resurrection had done for them—indeed, they would probably have got nowhere if they had not. It was equally reasonable that, in wrestling with the meaning of their faith, they should, on the basis of experience in preaching both to Jews and to Gentiles, find ways of explaining and expressing the faith which most effectively put it across to their contemporaries. But the framework of thought derived from the Old Testament is not necessarily the most suitable for the twentieth-century world; and ideas which were valid and central in their experience are not necessarily valid and central in ours. It is not reasonable to assume that the 'added' portions of the apostolic faith could be crystallized into established doctrines, handed on from age to age, and still remain as valid and vital nineteen centuries later.

To the orthodox Christian view, the teaching in the synoptic Gospels is, as an expression of the Christian faith, hopelessly incomplete. The apostles did not even put that teaching in the centre. Instead they focused attention on the authority of Jesus as Messiah and the saving power of faith in Him; and this was later developed as the saving power of the Cross. I am not concerned to discuss the efficacy or otherwise of this theology, nor the question of whether or not the apostles and the Church were right to make it the central theme. My point is that however appropriate it may have been then, it is not necessarily the right central theme for the twentieth century.

My first proposition, in Chapter 1, was that in matters of Christian faith and practice the teaching and example of Christ Himself should be our primary authority. I now come to the second proposition, which may not be new but which I think now deserves serious consideration: that the teaching of Christ, if it could be 'translated' into present-day terms more effectively than I can ever do, may well be a better twentieth-century expression of Christian faith than the early teaching of the apostles about Him. There is evidence in the synoptic Gospels that Jesus Himself considered it more important to do what He said than to call Him Lord.

12 Christ's Word for Today

A TIME OF DECISION

Mankind is at the crossroads. We live in an age of new horizons and new powers—powers that can be used either for good or for evil. This is a time of decision, and every one of you has a part to play in making that decision.

On the face of it, ordinary people don't seem to count for much. The world seems to be dominated by great nations and mass media, and controlled by the people who know how to manipulate money and power. But don't be misled: this is still God's world, although Man can make a mess of it, or even destroy it if he is foolish enough.

We are all part of God's creation. But God is not an absentee landlord sitting somewhere up in heaven. He is here, now, with you and in you. He is the mind behind the universe, the creative energy that made the distant star or the flower in your garden; yet His energy is focused in the lives of all who will receive Him. That is the good news about God: He works through ordinary people—the workman at the bench, the family in the modern semi, the peasant in an Indian village—these are God's chosen instruments. So forget everything else you ever thought about Him and enter into that tremendous truth.

GOOD NEWS FOR THE PEOPLE

My task is to make this known. It is good news for the underdog, the underfed, the underprivileged: good news for everyone who is held down by the powers that be, or pushed aside in the rat race, or shackled by the conventions of society. And believe me, it's dynamite. It won't fit into the accepted order of the establishment. It will come into conflict with the traditional churches when they lay down formal rules and dogmas, and with the laws of the State when it tries to regiment people to fit into its own pattern of power. The energy of God springs up within people and cannot be contained by any set of imposed rules, nor made acceptable to the world's authorities.

But don't misunderstand me. I am not preaching anarchism. The law still stands, though it is God's law, not man's. My aim is not to detract from it but to bring it to completion. Your response to accepted moral standards must be not to reject them but to go beyond them. The good news is not about a new kind of lawlessness but a new kind of man.

THE PEOPLE OF GOD

People who are God-centred have a different scale of values which are upside down compared with those of the world, and they find the secret of happiness in the joyful acceptance of those values. They don't strive after wealth but are content with what they have. They don't push themselves forward but find their satisfaction in the fulfilment of others. They never try to get their own back, but respond to evil with good, never delight in conflict, but make peace. They cannot ignore wrong but have a consuming passion for the victory of right—a singlemindedness of moral purpose. They stand by the cause of right to the point of suffering and persecution.

People like that are very close to God. They are the salt of the earth—the light of the world. Let your light shine like that, so that others will see the good you do and recognize your heavenly Father at work in you.

THE NEW MORALITY

Let me give you a few examples of what I mean by going beyond accepted standards of morality.

None of you in his right mind would dream of committing murder, but do you ever have murder in your heart? If you nurse anger against anyone you are slipping from grace and the love of God is not in you.

You know it is wrong to commit adultery—though even that commandment is being watered down nowadays. But you must not be content with merely refraining from the act of adultery—your standard should be absolute purity in mind as well as in body. By the same token you cannot accept divorce in the free and easy way that people do nowadays, as if a marriage can be broken just because it becomes difficult. For you the marriage bond must be completely binding, because the sacredness of marriage and family life is part of God's creative purpose. That principle is the foundation of a right relationship—both mental and physical—with the opposite sex.

Another example is the usual attitude to honesty. Most people are not worried about white lies, but would be ashamed to go back on their solemn word. But your honesty should not need reinforcing with solemn words or swearing in a court of law: you should be truthful at all times, and your integrity will make such things unnecessary and meaningless.

THE NEW RELATIONSHIPS

The same principle applies to personal relationships. It is commonly accepted that if someone hits you—figuratively or literally—you have a right to hit back. Indeed, the world despises the man who fails to hit back, and respects the one who does hit back with vigour. But you should not set yourself up against anyone who wrongs you: take hold of the situation and turn it round for good; make it an opportunity for creating a new relationship and turning an enemy into a friend.

Again, we are told often enough that 'charity begins at home', but never let your charity end there. You are to do good to your enemies, bless those who curse you and pray for those who wrong you. If you only do good to those who will do you good in return, what is special in that? And if you only give things to people who will give something back, what is the credit in that? God sends His good gifts for everybody, good and bad, and your love should be as wide as that. Your actions, like God's, should always be good actions, even in response to evil ones.

Don't make a show of your high principles. If you give generously, do it on the quiet so that no one knows about it. If you abstain from drink and gambling, don't make a song and dance about it, or set yourselves up as better than others. There are plenty of self-righteous people who do good with an eye to the gallery. No doubt they get a kick out of it—but your reward will be the knowledge that you have your heavenly Father's approval.

In the same spirit, don't sit in judgement on other people. Remember that you are vulnerable yourselves and people who live in glass houses should never throw stones. You look silly offering to extract a speck of dust from someone else's eye when you have a great plank in your own.

THE TRUE SECURITY

Don't put your trust in a big bank account, for 'where your treasure is, there will your heart be also.' Wealth is a positive hindrance to God-centred living, because the man who thinks money is all-important becomes a slave to it, and you cannot serve both God and money.

Indeed, you are not to worry about material things at all, not even essentials like food and clothing. If you really trust in God you should take such things in your stride, and turn your attention to the things that really matter—the things of the spirit. Look at the birds of the air: they have no bonuses or bank accounts and yet your heavenly Father feeds them. Look at the flowers in your garden: they never read the fashion magazines, yet they are more beautifully dressed than any fashion model. If God takes care of their clothing, how much more will he look after yours? So don't let your life be taken up with getting and spending. Above all, seek the indwelling presence of God, and the rest will take care of itself.

This is the focal point of my message, the treasure beyond price. The broad way of the world—the way of least resistance—leads to destruction. Only through this narrow gate can you enter into the joy of eternal life, and not many people are finding it.

LIFE IN THE PRESENCE OF GOD

If God is within you—'closer than breathing, nearer than hands and feet'—then you can keep in touch with Him all the time. You don't have to wait for a special time, or to go to Church, before you can pray. You can speak to Him at any time, or in the loneliness of your own room. Remember that He is eternal, creator of all things, but pray to Him simply about your everyday needs and difficulties. Ask His forgiveness for all you have done wrong, but always have a spirit of forgiveness in your own heart for any who may have wronged you.

You are to think of Him as your heavenly Father. He knows all your needs, knows all your sins, numbers the very hairs of your head. Don't be afraid to come to Him again and again for help and forgiveness—'Ask, and you will receive; seek, and you will find; knock, and the door will be opened to you.'

No matter what wrongs you may have done, if you are truly sorry your heavenly Father will receive you back into His family. But you must have the same forgiving spirit for others. Don't imagine that God is only interested in respectable, church-going people. He is even more concerned for the criminals and traitors and misfits whom the world dismisses as worthless—because they need Him most. If a farmer has a hundred sheep and one of them has got through the hedge and gone astray, he will leave all the others in the field and go off in search of the stray until he finds it; and when he finds it he will forget all the rest in his joy at finding the one that was lost. In the same way God is delighted over one bad man who makes good more than over ninety-nine people who are already good.

The life of the spirit does not end with the death of the body. That does not mean that after death you go into a sort of saintly replica of this life somewhere up in heaven, nor that you spend the rest of time in white robes singing endless psalms! But if you have lived this life in the presence of God your reward will be the joy of being for ever at home with your heavenly Father. In this world you will have persecution and suffering, but it is worth all that to gain the prize of eternal joy. To lose that prize is the worst thing that could happen to you.

QUALIFICATIONS FOR ETERNAL LIFE

What then are the qualifications needed for eternal life? The first is to put your trust in God. A little child puts complete trust in his mother, and psychologists will tell you that this trust is absolutely essential for proper growth, and is the base from which the child can explore new horizons and new experiences. So you must have a childlike trust in your heavenly Father as an essential beginning for spiritual growth.

The second is a change of heart. This means not only being sorry for wrongs you have done, but putting behind you all preconceived ideas and being ready to look in a new direction and adopt unfamiliar ways.

The third is humility of spirit, the readiness to sink self and look with fresh eyes at other people, with the kind of new scale of values I described to you before.

And the fourth is to do what you know to be right—to seek goodness above everything else; and this means a standard of goodness far beyond ordinary accepted ideas of decency.

The whole thing is summed up in the two great commandments, which are the same today as they always were: to love God with all your heart, and soul, and mind and strength; and to love your neighbour as yourself. And your 'neighbour' means not just the people next door, or your own family, friends or countrymen: it means anyone who is at hand and needs your help.

Helpfulness, then, is the acid test of your discipleship.

When you come to the end of your earthly life, this will be the supreme test of whether or not you are worthy to enter God's eternal presence. Have you been good to other people? If you have, you are in; if you haven't, you are out.

But remember that God looks on the inside, not on the outside, The world takes too much notice of outward appearance. When a firm decides to market a new product, they will spend a great deal of money on attractive packaging, because people may be more influenced by the package than they are by the goods inside. This may be harmless enough if it only applies to goods in the shops, but it can be serious if you have the same approach to more important things. When you go to Church, it is not the outward form, or ceremony, or solemn ritual that counts, but the inner worship of the heart, for God sees into the heart. And in everyday life, if you lay great store by keeping up with the Joneses or having the right kind of car in keeping with your profession, you are missing the really important things—the inner qualities of integrity and kindness and faith which come from having the rule of God in your life.

THE POWER OF FAITH

Faith is not just intellectual belief. Nor is it a milk and water thing. It is a mainspring of action—not an armchair but a power house. It is rather out of favour nowadays because we are so mechanistic in our interpretation of things, and we think of power in different terms.

We are accustomed to the marvels of modern science, and we see things done every day which fifty years ago would have been considered fantasy or science fiction. But don't imagine that scientific success excludes God. Whenever a man's sight is restored by a corneal graft, or a life saved by blood transfusion, or a child cured of yaws by a shot of penicillin, this is the finger of God at work. For God does not sit in some imaginary throne up in heaven. He is in the very stuff of life—its origin, its creative energy, its transforming power.

Because they see the increasing powers of physical science, people tend to belittle the power of the spirit, and the power of mind over matter. But for those who really know the presence of God and put their trust in him, faith works miracles. It can make you a whole, integrated personality, able to be and do all sorts of things you never dreamed of.

Faith does not take the place of science, nor compete with it. Sometimes it is an essential part of the scientific method, especially when men are reaching out to new discoveries. Sometimes it goes hand in hand with science, as every good G.P. knows. Sometimes it achieves spectacular results which seem to belong to a different dimension. But to those who know the reality of God these things are all of a piece because God is in them all.

THE GROWTH OF GOD'S EMPIRE

God-in-man is not only good news for the individual. It is also the answer to the challenge of evil and the troubles of the world. But God's empire is not to be imposed by Act of Parliament, nor brought about by resolutions at the United Nations; nor does it follow in the path of armies of 'liberation'. It grows—in people and through people.

Every man who wins the prize of God's presence in his own life becomes a centre of growth for God's empire in the world. When a farmer sows a field with wheat, some of it falls on stony ground and never takes root, and some of it is snapped up by the birds, but the seed which does take root grows and becomes fruitful and bears seed of its own. In the same way every man or woman who lives a dedicated life is scattering the seeds of truth. Some seeds never take root and are lost; some never survive the onslaught of materialism and selfishness; but some take root in other people's lives and then those who have received it will themselves do the spreading.

The world is on the edge of disaster and the challenge of evil is as strong as it ever was. God's empire does not grow by itself because each centre of growth is a free man or woman, free to choose good or evil, to do nothing or to dedicate a life to God. So it is up to you to scatter the seeds wherever you go. Let it be a chain reaction of good, spreading throughout the world. There is not much time. The way things are going, mankind will blow itself to pieces before long. If that happens those who have kept the faith will inherit the life of eternity.

Never underestimate the powers of evil. This battle between God's empire and the power of evil is in deadly earnest. If you accept the principles I have been teaching and live up to them, you will find yourself swimming against the tide. You may be up against your own family and friends and be cut off from those you love, for this thing takes priority even over family ties. You may be up against Church or State, and you may even have to give your life for your faith. Don't be afraid of those who can kill your body—they cannot kill your soul. Never compromise; never let the enemy lead you astray; if there is anything in your life that is dragging you down, tear it out ruthlessly no matter what the cost. Hold to your faith and keep right on to the end, and you will be rewarded with new life that is eternal.

If only the world could see the wonder of God's love! But nations are too busy striving for wealth and power. The rich nations are getting richer and the poor are getting poorer; and those who have wealth and resources, instead of using them to help others, are squandering them in the struggle for power. Their nuclear bombs and inter-continental missiles are works of the Devil, and if you put your faith in them you are trusting in the power of the Devil instead of your heavenly Father. This wickedness cannot go on forever. Some day someone will press the button. Then their affluent society will be smashed to pieces and the world which God created will be turned by man into a desert of death. Their boasted civilization will tumble in ruins about their ears, because when the time of decision came, they did not dare to choose the way of peace.